25 Quick FORMATIVE ASSESSMENTS
for a Differentiated Classroom

Judith Dodge

■SCHOLASTIC

New York • Toronto • London • Auckland • Sydney
Mexico City • New Delhi • Hong Kong • Buenos Aires

Introduction

■ ■ ■ ■ ■ ■ ■ ■ ■ ■ ■ ■ ■ ■ ■ ■

WHAT ARE FORMATIVE ASSESSMENTS AND WHY SHOULD WE USE THEM?

"Informative assessment isn't an end in itself, but the beginning of better instruction."

CAROL ANN TOMLINSON (2007/2008, P. 11)

Formative assessments are ongoing assessments, observations, summaries, and reviews that inform teacher instruction and provide students feedback on a daily basis (Fisher & Frey, 2007). While assessments are always crucial to the teaching and learning process, nowhere are they more important than in a differentiated classroom, where students of all levels of readiness sit side by side. Without the regular use of formative assessment, or checks for understanding, how are we to know what each student needs to be successful in our classroom? How else can we ensure we are addressing students' needs instead of simply teaching them what we *think* they need?

Traditionally, we have used assessments to measure how much our students have learned up to a particular point in time (Stiggins, 2007). This is what Rick Stiggins calls "assessment of learning" and what we use to see whether our students are meeting standards set by the state, the district, or the classroom teacher. These *summative assessments* are conducted after a unit or certain time period to determine how much learning has taken place.

Although Stiggins notes that assessments *of* learning are important if we are to ascribe grades to students and provide accountability, he urges teachers to focus more on assessment *for* learning. These types of assessment—*formative assessments*—support learning during the learning process.

Since formative assessments are considered part of the learning, they need not be graded as summative assessments (end-of-unit exams or quarterlies, for example) are. Rather, they serve as practice for students, just like a meaningful homework assignment (Chappuis & Chappuis, 2007/2008). They check for understanding along the way and guide teacher decision making about future instruction; they also provide feedback to students so they can improve their performance. Stiggins suggests "the student's role is to strive to understand what success looks like and to use each assessment to try to understand how to do better the next time." Formative assessments help us differentiate instruction and thus improve student achievement.

When I work with teachers during staff development, they often tell me they don't have time to assess students along the way. They fear sacrificing coverage and insist they must move on quickly. Yet in the rush to cover more, students are actually learning less. Without time to reflect on and interact meaningfully with new information, students are unlikely to retain much of what is "covered" in their classrooms.

Formative assessments, however, do not have to take an inordinate amount of time. While a few types (such as extended responses or essays) take considerably more time than others, many are quick and easy to use on a daily basis. On balance, the time they take from a lesson is well worth the information you gather and the retention students gain.

4

Using a Variety of Formative Assessments

The National Forum on Assessment (1995) suggests that assessment systems include opportunities for both individual and group work. To provide you with a comprehensive repertoire, I have labeled each assessment as Individual, Partner, Small Group, or Whole Class (see chart, page 11). Listening in on student partners or small-group conversations allows you to quickly identify problems or misconceptions, which you can address immediately. If you choose a group assessment activity, you will frequently want to follow it up with an individual one to more effectively pinpoint what each student needs. Often, the opportunity to work with others before working on their own leads students toward mastery. The group assessment process is part of the learning; don't feel you must grade it. The individual assessment that follows can remain ungraded, as well, although it will be most useful if you provide some feedback to the learner, perhaps in the form of a brief comment or, at the very least, a check, check-plus or check-minus, with a brief verbal explanation about what each symbol indicates (*You have mastered the skill, You need more practice,* etc.).

By varying the type of assessment you use over the course of the week, you can get a more accurate picture of what students know and understand, obtaining a "multiple-measure assessment 'window' into student understanding" (Ainsworth & Viegut, 2006). Using at least one formative assessment daily enables you to evaluate and assess the quality of the learning that is taking place in your classroom and answer these driving questions: *How is this student evolving as a learner? What can I do to assist this learner on his path to mastery?*

Types of Assessment Strategies

I have chosen a variety of quick ways for you to check for understanding and gather "evidence" of learning in your classroom. In this book, you will find four different types of formative assessments.

- **Summaries and Reflections** Students stop and reflect, make sense of what they have heard or read, derive personal meaning from their learning experiences, and/or increase their metacognitive skills. These require that students use content-specific language.

- **Lists, Charts, and Graphic Organizers** Students will organize information, make connections, and note relationships through the use of various graphic organizers.

- **Visual Representations of Information** Students will use both words and pictures to make connections and increase memory, facilitating retrieval of information later on. This "dual coding" helps teachers address classroom diversity, preferences in learning style, and different ways of "knowing."

- **Collaborative Activities** Students have the opportunity to move and/or communicate with others as they develop and demonstrate their understanding of concepts.

How to Use the Assessments in This Book

The quick formative assessments found within this book are designed for easy implementation in any classroom. Almost all can be used, with a little modification, throughout grades 3–8 and across the curriculum. A few are better for either younger or more sophisticated learners. Each strategy is labeled for easy identification by grade level on the list of strategies found on page 11.

You can choose any of the 25 quick assessments in this book to measure learning in your classroom. For each strategy, I will provide the following.

- ■ **Introduction** A description of the strategy and the relevant research behind it. I will explain how the strategy supports differentiated instruction.

- ■ **Step-by-Step Instructions** Steps for introducing and modeling the strategy for students

- ■ **Applications** Suggestions regarding what you can assess with the strategy

In addition, for many strategies you'll find:

- ■ **Tips for Tiering** Any ideas specific to the strategy for supporting struggling learners and challenging advanced learners that may not appear in the Introduction of this book

- ■ **TechConnect** Ideas for integrating technology with the formative assessment

- ■ **Reproducibles and/or Completed Samples of Student Work**

All reproducibles in the book are on the enclosed CD. I've also included variations of some forms that are only on the CD. See page 95 for a complete list of the CD contents.

EXIT CARDS

One of the easiest formative assessments is the Exit Card. Exit Cards are index cards (or sticky notes) that students hand to you, deposit in a box, or post on the door as they leave your classroom. On the Exit Card, your students have written their names and have responded to a question, solved a problem, or summarized their understanding after a particular learning experience. In a few short minutes, you can read the responses, sort them into groups (*students who have not yet mastered the skill, students who are ready to apply the skill, students who are ready to go ahead or to go deeper*), and use the data to inform the next day's or, even, that afternoon's instruction.

Feedback provided by the Exit Cards frequently leads to the formation of a needs-based group whose members require reteaching of the concept in a different way. It also identifies which of your students do not need to participate in your planned whole-group mini-lesson, because they are ready to be challenged at a greater level of complexity.

Several of the formative assessments contained in this book can be used as Exit Cards. In the table on page 11, I have placed an asterisk next to those assessments that you can use as an Exit Card to quickly sort and group students for subsequent instruction.

Keeping Track of the Data

When you use formative assessments, you must keep track of the data that you collect. The easiest way to observe and assess student growth is to walk around your room with a clipboard and sticky notes. As you notice acquisition of a new skill or confusion and struggle with a skill, record the student's name and jot down a brief comment. Consider keeping a folder for each child in which you insert any notes that you make on a daily basis. This process will help you focus on the needs of individual students when you confer with each child or develop lessons for your whole class.

Another way to keep track of the data is to use a class list such as the one on page 8. On this sheet, you can note specific skills and record how each student is doing. You can use a system of check-minus, check, and check-plus or the numbers 4, 3, 2, 1 to indicate student proficiency with the skill.

Differentiating Instruction in Response to Formative Assessments

Thomas R. Guskey suggests that for assessments to become an integral part of the instructional process, teachers need to change their approach in three important ways. They must "1) use assessments as sources of information for both students and teachers, 2) follow assessments with high-quality corrective instruction, and 3) give students second chances to demonstrate success" (2007).

Once you have assessed your learners, you must take action. You will be able to help your students achieve success by differentiating your instruction based on the information you have gathered. Ask yourself, "Who needs my attention now? Which students need a different approach? Which students are not learning anything new, because I haven't challenged them?" "Tiering" your activities for two or three levels of learners is usually what is called for after a review of assessment data. We must be prepared to provide both corrective activities and enrichment activities for those who need them. An important caveat to keep in mind, however, is that the follow-up, corrective instruction designed to help students must present concepts in new ways and engage students in different learning experiences that are more appropriate for them (Guskey, 2007/2008). Your challenge will be to find a new and different pathway to understanding. The best corrective activities involve a change in format, organization, or method of presentation (Guskey, 2007/2008).

After using any of the formative assessments contained in this book, you can choose from among the suggestions on page 9 to scaffold your struggling learners or challenge your advanced learners. The suggestions for struggling learners will help students during their "second-chance" learning on the road toward mastery. The suggestions for advanced learners will challenge those students who, in my opinion, are frequently forgotten in mixed-ability classrooms. With these easy adjustments to your lesson plans, you will be able to respond to the diverse readiness needs of students in your heterogeneous classroom.

Formative Assessment Data Collection

Assessment of: _____

4=Advanced
3=Proficient
2=Developing
1=Beginning

Students	List Specific Skills: Record 4, 3, 2, 1										

Now what? The next step . . .

Use the information gathered to design tiered activities.

See page 9 for ideas on how to tier follow-up learning activities.

25 Quick Formative Assessments for a Differentiated Classroom
© 2009 by Judith Dodge • Scholastic Teaching Resources

Designing Tiered Activities

Addressing Student Needs at Different Levels of Readiness

Scaffolding Struggling Learners

- Offer teacher direction (reteaching with a *different* method).
- Allow the student to work with a reading partner, study buddy, or learning partner. (Buddy-up an English language learner (ELL) with another student.) This will provide peer support for collaborative learning.
- Allow students to use class notes, textbooks, and/or other classroom resources to complete the task.
- Provide a model or exemplar (of a similar problem solved or a sample of the type of writing expected).
- Furnish step-by-step directions; break down the task.
- Provide hints or tips.
- Color-code different elements; highlight for focusing; provide "masks and markers" for focused attention on specific text.
- Provide sentence strips, sticky labels with terms, or manipulatives (plastic coins, Judy clocks, Unifix cubes, fraction tiles, number lines, algebraic tiles, calculators, etc.).
- Provide a partially completed graphic organizer or outline.
- Provide out-of-sequence steps for students to reorganize.
- Provide a cloze (fill-in-the-blank) paragraph (with or without a word box) for students whose language is extremely limited or for those who struggle with grapho-motor skills.
- Give a framed paragraph or essay (with sentence starters to help organize the writing).
- Provide guided questions.
- Supply a word bank and definitions.
- Support with visuals, diagrams, or pictures.
- Provide words on labels for students to simply pull off and place appropriately.
- Allow additional time.

Challenging Advanced Learners

- Design activities that are more complex, abstract, independent, and/or multistep.
- Pose a challenge question or task that requires them to think beyond the concrete and obvious response (from the newly learned material) to more abstract ideas and new use of the information.
- Require more complex expression of ideas: different types of sentences, synonyms, more than one adjective or action (verb) to describe what's happening.
- Require that metaphors and similes, idiomatic expressions, or specific literary elements be included in their writing.
- Ask students to make text-to-text and text-to-world connections (more abstract than text-to-self connections).
- Require students to note relationships and point out connections among ideas: compare and contrast; cause and effect; problem and solution; sequence, steps, or change over time; advantages and disadvantages; benefits; etc.
- Ask students to tell the story from a different point of view.
- Ask students to place themselves into the story or time period and write from the first-person point of view.
- Ask students to consider "What if?" scenarios.
- Provide multistep math problems.
- Include distracters.
- Do not provide a visual prompt.
- Ask students to suggest tips or hints that would help others who struggle to make sense of the information
- Provide a problem or model that does not work; have students problem-solve.
- Have students create their own pattern, graph, experiment, word problem, scenario, story, poem, etc.
- Have students use the information in a completely new way (*Design an awareness campaign about . . .* ; *Create a flier to inform . . .* ; *Write/give a speech to convince . . .* ; *Write an article to educate . . .* ; *Write an ad to warn others about . . .* ; *Design a program to solve the problem of . . . .*)

Gathering Multiple Sources of Evidence

In differentiated classrooms everywhere, a resounding mantra is "Fair is not equal; fair is getting what you need." Assessments enable us to determine what students need. But for our assessments to be accurate, we need multiple measures of student understanding. We need evidence gathered over time in different ways to evaluate how effective the teaching and learning process has been. Tomlinson and McTighe (2006) suggest that when we gather a "photo album" rather than a "snapshot" of our students, we can differentiate instruction based on a more accurate evaluation of our students' learning needs.

I wish you success as you gather your own "photo album" of your students and choose from a variety of reflective, unique, and engaging assessment tools. This book offers you an "assessment tool kit" to choose from as you create a classroom that is continually more responsive to the needs of your diverse learners. These assessments will provide you and your students "evidence" of their learning and help them on their journey to greater achievement in school.

Response to Intervention (RTI)

With the reauthorization of the Individuals with Disabilities Education Act (IDEA, 2004) under No Child Left Behind, schools are searching for ways to implement the newly required Response to Intervention (RTI) model. This new way of delivering intervention to struggling students encompasses a three-tiered model.

Tier 1 interventions include monitoring at-risk students within the general education classroom, ensuring that each student has access to a high-quality education that is matched to his or her needs. RTI focuses on improving academic achievement by using scientifically based instructional practices.

According to the National Association of State Directors of Special Education (2005), Tier 1 strategies encompass "alternative assessment which utilizes quality interventions matched to student needs, coupled with formative evaluation to obtain data over time to make critical educational decisions." Not to be confused with tiered activities, which are a cornerstone of a differentiated classroom (where one concept is taught at two or three levels of readiness), Tier I activities are any of the in-class interventions classroom teachers provide to assess and monitor their at-risk students.

The evidence-based formative assessments provided in this book are excellent methods for classroom teachers to measure the progress of their Tier 1 students.

We gather a snapshot rather than a photo album.

25 Quick Formative Assessments
Quick Reference

Section 1   SUMMARIES & REFLECTIONS | VERBAL-LINGUISTIC & INTERPERSONAL

Gr. 3–5	Gr. 6–8	I·P·G·C	Assessments	TechConnect	Page #
✓	✓	I·P·G·C	▪ Dry-Erase Boards	✓	13
✓	✓	I	▪ QuickWrite*	✓	15
✓	✓	I	▪ WriteAbout*	✓	16
✓	✓	I	▪ S-O-S Summary*		19
✓	✓	I	▪ 3-2-1 Summarizer*		22
✓	✓	I	▪ My Opinions Journal	✓	25
	✓	I	▪ My Textbook Page	✓	28
	✓	G·I	▪ FactStorming	✓	32

*Can be used as Exit Cards

I–Individual
P–Partner
C–Whole Class
G–Small Group

Section 2   LISTS, CHARTS, AND GRAPHIC ORGANIZERS | LOGICAL-MATHEMATICAL

Gr. 3–5	Gr. 6–8	I·P·G·C	Assessments	TechConnect	Page #
✓	✓	I	▪ My Top Ten List*		38
✓	✓	I·P·G	▪ Matrix		41
✓	✓	I	▪ Noting What I've Learned		44
✓	✓	I·P·G	▪ List-Group-Label (LGL)		47
✓	✓	I·P·G	▪ Web Wind-Up	✓	50

Section 3   VISUAL REPRESENTATIONS OF INFORMATION | SPATIAL

Gr. 3–5	Gr. 6–8	I·P·G·C	Assessments	TechConnect	Page #
✓		I	▪ Picture Note Making*	✓	53
✓	✓	I·G	▪ QuickWrite/QuickDraw!*		56
✓	✓	I	▪ Unit Collage	✓	59
✓	✓	I	▪ Photo Finish	✓	63
✓	✓	I	▪ Filming the Ideas	✓	67
✓	✓	I	▪ Flipbooks	✓	73
✓	✓	I	▪ SmartCards*	✓	76

Section 4   COLLABORATIVE ACTIVITIES | KINESTHETIC & INTERPERSONAL

Gr. 3–5	Gr. 6–8	I·P·G·C	Assessments	TechConnect	Page #
✓	✓	P	▪ Turn 'n' Talk	✓	80
	✓	P·G	▪ Headline News! Summary	✓	82
✓	✓	C	▪ Four More!		85
✓	✓	C	▪ Find Someone Who … Review		91
✓	✓	G·C	▪ Carousel Brainstorming	✓	94

Section 1

Summaries and Reflections

The strategies that follow are summaries and written reflections. Relying heavily on verbal-linguistic skills and focusing mostly on intrapersonal intelligence, students are asked to reflect upon their own learning. They must reorganize information to make meaning for themselves. Brooks and Brooks (cited in McLaughlin & Vogt, 2000) note that from a constructivist point of view, learning is understood as a process that incorporates concrete experience, collaborative discourse, and reflection. Following are eight strategies that invite students to summarize and reflect after their learning experiences.

Dry-Erase Boards

Using dry-erase boards has been a standard strategy in classrooms where teachers encourage consistent student engagement. However, there are many classrooms where dry-erase boards sit on shelves or in closets gathering dust, remnants of a forgotten, or underused, technique for energizing classrooms. Let me share an important reason for digging them out and dusting them off.

Assessment is immediate with the use of a dry-erase board. When students raise their boards during class to offer responses to a question or problem, you get on-the-spot information. You can see if students are incorporating new knowledge, and which areas, if any, are presenting confusion. Depending upon your assessment of student understanding, you can instantly change the direction of your lesson or reteach a part of it.

Step-by-Step

1. If you have a class set of dry-erase boards, have two students pass one out to each classmate. This assigned job can rotate and can include collecting them at the end of the day and, occasionally, cleaning them of any remaining ink.

2. As students record and illustrate on the boards, pass among the desks, assessing student understanding. You might carry a clipboard to make notes about misconceptions or different ideas for sharing with students at the end of the activity.

Applications

Dry-erase boards can be used for any subject. They are, however, particularly useful for math, language arts, and foreign-language review, practice, and enrichment. See page 14 for a sample lesson in language arts.

The dry-erase board is flexible and ideal for use in a differentiated classroom. Among the myriad tasks you can design for dry-erase boards are answering questions, solving math problems, illustrating concepts, generating lists, composing sketches, and creating graphic organizers.

Whenever you feel the need to reengage your learners, you can create a brief activity with the dry-erase boards. You can use them from time to time throughout the day, for short practice, or for reflection. They can be used for warm-ups, homework review, or guided practice. They can be used by individual students, partners, or small groups. Visual learners are aided by the use of images and colors. Tactile-kinesthetic learners are supported by the physicality of writing or drawing, raising the boards, and the interactive environment they create.

You can use the boards as "Entrance Cards," on which students write or draw something that makes a connection to the previous day's lesson. This practice is effective in activating prior knowledge, and I've found it to be highly motivating as well.

Language Arts: EXPANDING SENTENCES

This activity will encourage students to write fuller, richer sentences.

- First, have students write a simple sentence on their board—for example, "Damien runs" or "Mary studies."
- Then, pull one card at a time from a set of cards with the following words written on them: *How? Where? When? With whom? Why?*

- As you pull one card at a time from the box, direct students to erase and rewrite their sentence to include the new information.
- Have two or three students share their sentences after each rewriting.

TechConnect

The makers of SMART Board technology have created a new gadget that allows for on-the-spot assessment. These interactive clickers, or Senteos, allow the teacher to prepare an "Ask the Audience" portion of a lesson to instantly measure and view graphs of student understanding.

For more info: www.smarttech.com (search: Senteo).

Using the free Web tool SurveyMonkey to assess students is another option. Unlike the handheld devices, SurveyMonkey doesn't provide instant access to information. However, the results can be retrieved from the Web site or stored for later use.

A tutorial for SurveyMonkey can be found at http://www.surveymonkey.com/Home_Videos.aspx.

Tips for Making Your Own Dry-Erase Boards!

There are many teacher stores and online distributors that sell class sets of individual dry-erase boards or paddle dry-erase boards (with handles for easier student use). Do an Internet search for "dry-erase boards" and you'll find thousands.

Most teachers, however, have budgetary constraints and find that class sets are too expensive for them to purchase (up to $100 per set). Instead, they make their own. It's easy. Go to a home improvement store and purchase one sheet of shower board—this is the material that is placed behind the tiles in a shower. It comes in 8' x 4' sheets and is white and shiny. One board costs around ten dollars. Many teachers have reported in online blogs that if you tell the salesperson that you are a teacher, he or she will accommodate you by cutting the board into 12" x 12" individual boards.

After having the board cut into the smaller size, cover the edges with duct tape. Ask your students to bring in old clean socks to serve as erasers. You will have to supply dry-erase pens, which can last the year, if properly taken care of (remind students to replace caps immediately when not in use).

After a while, the ink leaves marks that are hard to remove from the shower board. I found an excellent idea online from a teacher who suggested treating the boards with car wax before using them to help keep marks from becoming permanent. There are many products that can be used every once in a while to completely clean the boards. The savings incurred by making the boards yourself is worth the occasional time you or your students will need to clean them thoroughly.

25 Quick Formative Assessments for a Differentiated Classroom • © 2009 by Judith Dodge • Scholastic Teaching Resources

QuickWrite

A QuickWrite is a brief, timed writing activity. Giving students two or three minutes to reflect on and summarize their learning in writing allows them to make sense of what they have been studying.

Step-by-Step

1. Either midway through a lesson or at the end, provide students with a large sticky note, an index card, or a half-sheet of paper.

2. Advise students that they will have two (or three) minutes to reflect on what they have just learned and write about it.

3. State the prompt you want students to respond to. You may pose a question, ask for a summary of the content, require a list of steps, ask for an analysis of the work, or request the use of specific content-area vocabulary in a wrap-up of the topic under study. The more specific the prompt, the better the response.

4. Have a few students share their reflections with the class. Alternatively, you can collect the QuickWrites as Exit Cards.

Applications

A series of QuickWrites can be kept in a journal, allowing students to revisit what they have learned over time. You can collect the journals periodically and provide written feedback to your students.

TechConnect

Have students create a "TalkAbout" instead of a Quick-Write. Using a microphone connected to a computer and the free audio-capturing software that comes with Windows (Start/Programs/Accessories/Entertainment/ Sound Recorder), students will record their responses to the prompts instead of writing them. For students in a differentiated classroom who would find it easier to speak than to write, this option would provide an appropriate alternative assessment.

■ For about $50, teachers can purchase a Webcam to attach to the computer so students can videotape themselves providing the summary.

WriteAbout

Research has shown that summarization yields some of the greatest leaps in comprehension and long-term retention of information (Wormeli, 2005). A WriteAbout is a concrete tool for summarization in which students use key vocabulary terms (the language of the content area) to synthesize their understanding in a paragraph as well as represent key ideas graphically. Combining both verbal-linguistic and spatial intelligences, this assessment tool is a favorite of many students.

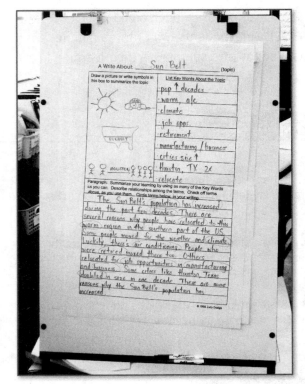

Debra Steinroder models a WriteAbout for her fifth-grade students using a poster-size version of a WriteAbout.

Step-by-Step

1. At the end of your lesson, provide a WriteAbout sheet to students (page 18).
(TIP: If you photocopy these pages on colored paper, they will be easy to find later when needed for studying.)

2. Model for the class how you would complete a WriteAbout. Depending upon the grade of your students, you may need to model several times. Brainstorm key words and draw a picture to represent the main idea.

3. Demonstrate how to write a summary using the key words on the list. Show students how you check off the terms as you use them and circle them in your writing.

4. Let partners talk and complete a WriteAbout together.

5. After a few practice opportunities with a partner, students should be ready to complete a WriteAbout on their own.

6. Collect this assessment and provide feedback to students. Provide a simple check or check-plus to indicate the individual's level of mastery. Share with your class what a check or check-plus means. (*A check means that you understand most of the terms and ideas, but still have to master others. Please notice any circles, question marks, or questions that I have written on your paper to help guide your next steps in learning.*)

7. Plan your instruction for the next day so that it fills any gaps in class understanding and/or includes flexible grouping for a follow-up tiered activity.

The WriteAbout is also a useful tool for homework. It provides an opportunity for students to synthesize the key understandings of the day's lesson.

Keep in mind, however, that this assessment is designed for a single concept within a larger unit. Don't use it, for example, to see what students have learned about the Civil War. Use it to see what they have learned about the Underground Railroad, the advantages held by the North or South, or Reconstruction after the war.

Teachers have used the WriteAbout paragraphs successfully with their "Expert Groups" in a Jigsaw review activity (See Dodge, 2005 for a more detailed explanation about the Jigsaw Activity.) Briefly, students are assigned a Home Base Group and each is given a different subtopic, question, reading, or problem to complete. They then move into Expert Groups to work with others given the same assignment. There, each student completes his own Write-About. When he/she returns to the original Home Base Group, each Expert contributes his/her piece to the group's poster on the whole topic. This poster or product represents a group assessment. To check for individual understanding, follow up with several short-response questions.

TechConnect

Using a software program like Kid Pix or the free paint tool that comes with Windows, students can draw the pictures, symbols, or steps. Then, using the paint tool found in either program, they can write their paragraph.

Tips for Tiering!

In addition to the ideas on page 9, consider the following.

To support struggling learners: Duplicate the Write-About template with the vocabulary terms already printed on it. (Provide definitions, if you feel they are necessary)

A WriteAbout: Animal Adaptations (Topic)

Draw a picture or write symbols in this box to summarize the topic

List Key Words About the Topic
adaptations ✓
survive ✓
environment ✓
finding food ✓
brown bear ✓
penguin ✓
having shelter ✓
pocket gopher ✓

Paragraph: Summarize your learning by using the terms above. Be sure to check off terms above, as you use them. Circle terms below, in your writing.

Adaptations are a part of behavior and the ways animals survive in their environment like for finding food. Brown bear's adaptation for finding food is their sharp claws, and big teeth. For a penguin it's the big flippers. Another adaptation is having shelter. A pocket gopher gets shelter by using its claws to dig holes.

© 2000 Judy Dodge

Students use A WriteAbout to help them process the information they have been learning in a unit on animal adaptations. They check off the vocabulary terms and circle them in their writing as they use the key words in context. (This template is available on the CD.)

Write About

Name _____ Date _____

Topic _____

Draw a picture or write symbols in this box to summarize the topic	**List Key Words** about the topic
	❏ _____
	❏ _____
	❏ _____
	❏ _____
	❏ _____
	❏ _____
	❏ _____
	❏ _____
	❏ _____

Paragraph: Summarize your learning by using the terms above in a paragraph about the topic. Check off the terms as you use them. Then circle the terms in your paragraph.

_____

_____

_____

_____

_____

_____

_____

_____

_____

_____

S-O-S Summary

An S-O-S Summary is an assessment that can be used at any point in a lesson. The teacher presents a *statement* (S), asks the student's *opinion* (O) (whether the student agrees or disagrees with the statement), and asks the student to *support* (S) his or her opinion with evidence. This summary can be used before or during a unit to assess student attitudes, beliefs, and knowledge about a topic. It can be used at points throughout a unit or lesson to assess what students are coming to understand about the topic. And it can be used at the end of a unit to see if attitudes and beliefs have been influenced or changed as a result of new learning.

S-O-S

- Read the following **s**tatement: _____
   What does it mean?

- What's your **o**pinion?
   Circle one: I agree   I disagree

- **S**upport your opinion with evidence (facts, data, reasons, examples, etc.).

S-O-S Summary

Given this statement: Cara Landry is a truthful reporter.

What does it mean? Cara Landry only reports the truth.

What's your opinion?   Circle one: (I agree)   I disagree

Support your opinion with evidence (facts, reasons, examples, etc.)
- she investagated on the topics before she puts it in her newspaper
- if she knew information wasn't true she wouldn't publish it
- her newspapers never told a lie

S-O-S Summary

Given this statement: Mr. Larson is hard working.

What does it mean? Mr. Larson works hard.

What's your opinion?   Circle one: I agree   (I disagree)

Support your opinion with evidence (facts, reasons, examples, etc.)
- he didn't teach
- he drinks coffee and sits at his desk
- doesn't care what the kids in his class are doing

This fifth grade student is using the S-O-S Summary to practice writing an English Language Arts essay on characterization—without all of the writing. Reacting to the given statement, she provides her opinion with brief, bulleted responses, supporting her opinion with evidence. (This template is available on the CD.)

Step-by-Step

1. Provide students with an S-O-S Summary sheet (page 21).

2. Write a statement (not a question!) on the board for students to copy. This activity works best when the statement is one which can be argued from two points of view (see sample statements in box below).

3. Give students five minutes to agree or disagree with the statement by listing facts, data, reasons, examples, and so on that they have learned from class discussion, reading, or media presentations.

4. Collect the S-O-S Summary sheet to assess student understanding.

5. Make decisions about the next day's instruction.

Applications

The S-O-S Summary is excellent practice for essay writing without all of the writing. It helps students choose a point of view and support it with evidence presented in brief bulleted points. Teachers can use it frequently because it requires much less time than an essay—both to write and to assess.

The S-O-S Summary is also good practice for students who are required to complete DBQs (document-based questions) in social studies, write critical-lens essays in English Language Arts, or ponder ethical dilemmas in science. Each of these tasks requires students to take a stand on a particular issue and support their point of view with evidence, facts, and examples.

Sample Statements

- The main character is a hero.
- Recycling is not necessary in our community.
- If you are young, it's not important to have good health habits.
- The city is the best place to live.
- The Industrial Revolution produced only positive effects on society.
- You don't need to know math to live comfortably in the world.

Tips for Tiering!

In addition to the ideas on page 9, consider the following.

To challenge advanced learners: If you have a mature class, capable of independent, critical thinking, you can make this activity more complex. Ask half of the class to agree with the statement and the other half to disagree with it; have students complete an S-O-S Summary from their assigned viewpoint. Then hold a debate. Have the two groups stand on opposite sides of the room with their S-O-S Summary in hand and encourage the two sides to defend their opinions orally by using all of the facts, data, and examples they have written. Then, ask students to return to their seats and write the very best argument they can for the opposite viewpoint. This is an excellent exercise for developing listening skills; arguing from a particular viewpoint; and deconstructing conflicts in literature, history, and everyday life.

S-O-S Summary

Name _____ Date _____

Read the following **s**tatement: _____

_____

_____

What does it mean? _____

_____

_____

What's your **o**pinion?   Circle one: I agree   I disagree

Support your opinion with evidence (facts, reasons, examples, etc.).

- ■
- ■
- ■

Name _____ Date _____

Read the following **s**tatement: _____

_____

_____

What does it mean? _____

_____

_____

What's your **o**pinion?   Circle one: I agree   I disagree

Support your opinion with evidence (facts, reasons, examples, etc.).

- ■
- ■
- ■

3-2-1 Summarizer

A 3-2-1 Summarizer is a strategy for closure at the end of a lesson. The numbers refer to how many of each kind of summary statement or response you require students to provide. For example, you might ask students to record:

- **3 facts** they've learned
- **2 questions** they have or wonder about
- **1 personal connection** they can make to the information

As students pause for a few minutes to consider their learning, they are given a chance to reflect, organize their thoughts, summarize, prioritize important ideas, and, therefore, move the information into long-term memory.

Step-by-Step

1. At the end of your lesson, hand students a 3-2-1 Summarizer (page 24) or have them copy one from the board.

2. Ask students to reflect upon the lesson and respond to your prompts. The more focused the prompts, the better the assessment will be. A generic prompt like "List three things you learned today" will not provide you with as good an assessment as "State three causes of the Civil War."

3. Collect the 3-2-1 Summarizer as students leave the classroom or ask students to deposit them in a box specifically marked "Exit Cards." (Tell students, "Today's Exit Card is your 3-2-1 Summarizer.")

Applications

The type of information that you ask for can be adapted to any topic or content area.

Social Studies:

- **3** *Contributions* of Greek civilization
- **2** *Ways* the Greek economy differed from the Egyptian economy
- **1** *Way* the geography of Greece influenced Greek life

English Language Arts:

- **3** *Examples* of prejudice in the book
- **2** *Instances* that show how the main character's prejudiced views have changed
- **1** *Real-life situation* in which you were affected by or witnessed prejudice

Science:

- **3** *Parts (and functions)* of a plant
- **2** *Ways* to keep plants healthy
- **1** *Way* Earth would be affected if there were no plants

Math:

- **3** *Strategies* for solving word problems
- **2** *Important things to look for* when solving word problems
- **1** *Solution* to a provided word problem

Teachers in one district I worked in modified this strategy to raise the level of thinking required. Integrating Bloom's Taxonomy into the three types of prompts, they suggested that "3" represent low-level knowledge/comprehension prompts, that "2" represent middle-level application/analysis prompts, and that "1" represent high-level synthesis/evaluation prompts. See page 23 for an example of integrating Bloom's Taxonomy into the 3-2-1 Summarizer.

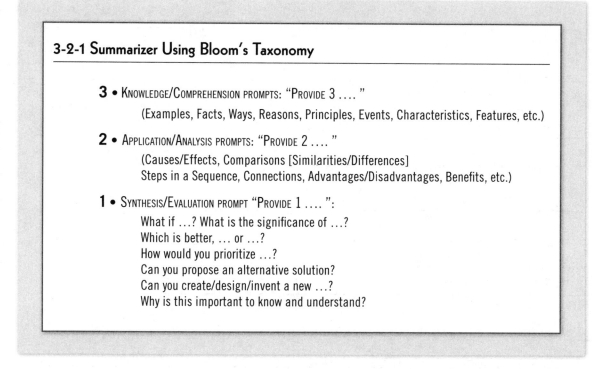

3-2-1 Summarizer Using Bloom's Taxonomy

3 • KNOWLEDGE/COMPREHENSION PROMPTS: "PROVIDE 3 ...."

(Examples, Facts, Ways, Reasons, Principles, Events, Characteristics, Features, etc.)

2 • APPLICATION/ANALYSIS PROMPTS: "PROVIDE 2 ...."

(Causes/Effects, Comparisons [Similarities/Differences]
Steps in a Sequence, Connections, Advantages/Disadvantages, Benefits, etc.)

1 • SYNTHESIS/EVALUATION PROMPT "PROVIDE 1 .... ":

What if ...? What is the significance of ...?
Which is better, ... or ...?
How would you prioritize ...?
Can you propose an alternative solution?
Can you create/design/invent a new ...?
Why is this important to know and understand?

Another variation of the 3-2-1 format is used in reading. Using the Question-Answer Relationship, or QAR (Raphael, 1986), teachers of reading can have students focus on four basic question-answer relationships: "Right There" questions (the answer is found in one sentence); "Think and Search" questions (the answer is found in more than one place; the reader needs to put ideas together); "Author and Me" questions (the answer is not in the text, but you need to think about what the author has said in order to respond); "On My Own" questions (the answer relies on your background knowledge of a topic, not the text).

A 3-2-1 Summarizer Using QAR

■ **Provide 3** Right There questions for students to answer:

How many ...?
Who is ...?
Where did ...?

■ **Provide 2** Think and Search questions for students to answer:

What is the main idea of this passage?
Why do you think ...?
What examples can you find of ...?
Compare and contrast ...

■ **Provide 1** Author and Me or On My Own question for students to answer:

The author implies ...
The speaker's attitude is ...
In your opinion ...
Describe a time when you ...

3-2-1 Summarizer

Name _____ Date _____

3 ■ _____
_____
_____
_____

■ _____
_____
_____
_____

■ _____
_____
_____
_____

2 ■ _____
_____
_____
_____

■ _____
_____
_____
_____

1 ■ _____
_____
_____
_____

My Opinions Journal

Reflection is critical to deep understanding. The learner must ask, "Does this make sense?" (Sousa, 2001). As students grapple with key ideas through discussion and writing, they make sense of what they are learning. The new information needs to fit into what they know, so the learners must make connections between what they already know and understand and what they are presently learning. David Sousa suggests that students must also find *meaning*, which he describes as "relevance," in the information. When we ask students to record their opinions and elaborate by making connections, we are providing opportunities for them to personalize their learning and find more relevance and meaning in their studies. The great payoff for this type of reflection is that if the information makes sense and has meaning for the learner, it is more likely to be remembered.

My Opinions Journal provides a vehicle for students to record their beliefs as they "come to know" (Atwell, 1990) and find deep meaning in what they are learning. It gives students practice in forming an opinion, supporting it with evidence, and communicating it to others. You can use My Opinions Journal as an assessment and a window into the minds of your students. Over time, the journals will become reflections of the growth of your learners and a record of how they are evolving.

Step-by-Step

1. Provide students with a small journal notebook (or a booklet made of lined paper). This "journal" can be a section of your students' notebook or you can store the journal notebooks in a crate in your classroom. (Have one student hand them out and another collect them on the days that you plan to use them.)

2. At the beginning of a unit, provide sentence starters like the following to activate prior knowledge:

In my opinion, _____ leads to _____
(**Example:** In my opinion, *prejudice* leads to _____)

I believe _____ is important because _____
(**Example:** I believe *protecting endangered species* is important because _____)

I think _____ is necessary because _____
(**Example:** I think *democracy* is necessary because _____)

I feel it is important to understand _____ because _____ (**Example:** I feel it is important to understand *fractions* because _____)

Model several times how you write a journal entry based on a prompt, until students are comfortable with the process (see example on page 26).

3. After modeling an example for the class, engage students in a *shared* writing by providing them with an opening statement (using sentence starters like those found in step 2), and having them work together to contribute support and evidence to back up the stated opinion.

4. Once students are comfortable with this format, stop periodically throughout a unit or activity and ask students to form an opinion about a particular concept, character, statement, or issue—and record it in their My Opinions Journal.

5. Collect the journals from time to time to provide feedback. Many teachers choose a day when students are busy working independently on an activity to read through the journals and hold mini-conferences with a few students. Others collect and read the journals, a few at a time, and offer students feedback in the form of brief written comments.

In addition to the ideas on page 9, consider the following.

To challenge advanced learners: Ask these students …

- What connections can you make from today's lesson to something else we've learned previously?
- What connections can you make to a different subject or discipline?

TechConnect

A blog is the perfect online publishing tool to encourage student communication about their opinions and to assess student understanding. Developed specifically for classroom use, Blog-meister.com is a safe space that requires teacher approval for all postings.

For more info: www.classblogmeister.com.

How to Write a Journal Entry

The class has identified many big ideas about the industrialization of the 1900s, including: *Industrialization had a negative impact on Americans.*

Model for students how they might respond in their My Opinions Journal to that big idea:

- I believe that industrialization during the early 1900s had a negative impact on Americans. As workers shifted from rural to urban life, their life in the cities consisted of run-down tenements and crowded living space. Crowding helped spread disease. Often, there were inadequate water and sanitation facilities. Fires broke out in the crowded tenements. Children worked in factories instead of going to school. I don't think industrialization helped families enough.

My Opinions Journal

Name _____ Date _____

Topic or Unit _____

Big Idea _____

_____

_____

_____

Use one of the sentence stems below (or choose your own) to respond to the "big idea" above:

- In my opinion, _____ leads to _____.
- I believe _____ is beneficial/dangerous because _____.
- I think _____ is necessary/important because_____.

- I feel it is important to _____ because _____.
- I used to believe/think/feel _____, but now I believe/think/feel _____ because _____.

_____

_____

_____

_____

_____

_____

_____

_____

_____

_____

_____

_____

_____

My Textbook Page

As part of a yearlong project, have students create a student-generated "textbook" of their own for your curriculum. Completing one page at a time, at intervals of about every other week, students will compile this study guide as part of their required homework. You will be able to use these pages to assess student understanding of a topic.

My Textbook Pages should be assigned after your class has explored an important concept. By summarizing main ideas, noting important vocabulary, explaining key concepts in their own words, and suggesting tips and hints for understanding the information, students will make the information their own. Kept in a three-ring binder, the individual student textbook that is created becomes the proud possession of each student and serves as an excellent study tool. Studying for midterms, finals, and other assessments becomes much easier when students have their own summaries and examples to review.

Step-by-Step

1. Photocopy My Social Studies or My Math Textbook Page (page 30 or 31) and distribute to students.

2. Model how to complete a sample textbook page on a topic you have just covered. Ask students for help in creating tips and hints. Show students how they can use colors, arrows, circles, and boxes to make the steps and examples clearer to the reader (see sample on page 29).

3. Assign students to work on My Textbook Page together the next day. They share ideas, but each student completes a page.

4. Ask students to complete their page for homework the following day.

5. Collect the pages you assign as homework to assess student understanding. Review and provide feedback to students on their textbook pages.

6. Ask students permission to keep two or three of the best examples to show as exemplars the next time you assign a textbook page.

Note: A My Science Textbook page is included on the CD.

Applications

Social studies and science teachers sometimes prefer that students contribute to a Class-Generated Student Textbook (see Tips for Tiering! page 29) on one big topic. A class book on the Revolutionary War, for example, might include pages from different students on various subtopics: British actions against the colonies, spies against Britain, the Loyalists versus the Patriots, events leading to the revolution, and so on.

You can put spiral bindings on these pages and save the books from year to year. These student-written books can be advance organizers for future classes to read. They will help students to learn the new material by providing a context and prior knowledge before you begin a new unit.

My *Social Studies* Textbook Page

Concept/Topic: ___The Louisiana Purchase___

Description/Summary of the Topic:	Key Vocabulary Terms/Definitions/Examples:
The Louisiana Purchase is considered the biggest bargain in American history. The French sold it cheaply to the U.S. It doubled the size of the United States.	• debt • territory • expedition • treaty

Important Historical Figures & Their Contributions:	Historical Developments/Key Events/Timeline:
Napoleon - French Leader T. Jefferson - U.S. President Lewis + Clark - explorers Sacajawea - Native American guide	1803 - Louisiana Purchase 1804 - Lewis + Clark begin their expedition 1805 - reach Pacific Ocean 1806 - travel back to St. Louis

Geographic/Economic Factors to Consider:	Cause-Effect Relationships:
US farmers worry that the French + Spanish might block their trade access at the French port of N. Orleans. Americans in the east want to move west to find more farmland	① French government needed money, so US bought land for $15 million ② The purchase doubles the size of the US ③ The purchase assures US of free navigation of the Mississippi ④ Questions about new land led to Lewis + Clark's journey

Name___Debra___ Date_____

This student synthesizes her learning on the topic of the Louisiana Purchase into a one-page summary for her student-generated textbook.

TechConnect

A wiki is a free online space for writing or publishing a document. Anyone can contribute, edit, or revise the document. Therefore, creating a class wiki on any topic, concept, or theme presents an exciting opportunity for all students to be involved in the publication. Developing a student wiki is the perfect place to create a Class-Generated Textbook Page. For teachers new to wikis, check out these sites:

http://writingwiki.org
Note: click on For Teachers New to Wikis on right side of screen

http://www.wikispaces.com

http://pbwiki.com

Tips for Tiering!

In addition to the ideas on page 9, consider the following.

To challenge advanced learners: Ask advanced students to compile a Class-Generated Student Textbook. Keep this textbook in your possession and use it during extra-help sessions with students who are struggling with a concept or who need additional review on a topic. Written in student language, these class books often make difficult material more accessible to struggling learners.

My Social Studies Textbook Page

Name _____ Date _____

Concept/Topic _____

Description/Summary of the Topic:	Key Vocabulary Terms:
Important Historical Figures and Their Contributions:	Historical Developments/Key Events:
Geography/Economy:	Achievements:

My Math Textbook Page

Name _____ Date _____

Concept/Topic _____

Description/Summary of the Concept:	Examples/Step-by-Step Instructions:
Hints/Tips: Keep in mind … Remember to …	The most important things to understand about this concept are:
How this concept relates to other concepts we've studied:	URLs to find out more and to practice:

FactStorming

FactStorming is a summarization activity that begins as a whole-class review and leads to individuals, pairs, or small groups reworking the information to make it their own. Engaging students in a class brainstorm or "idea splash" is just the first step in this review or assessment activity. It involves much more than just identifying a low-level list of "facts."

Toward the end of a unit, generate and record a student-made list of facts, events, movements, ideas, principles, factors, concepts, attributes, character-istics, documents, themes, characters, groups, key figures, and so forth about the topic you have been studying. Then offer a choice of high-level writing activities that provide different ways for students to organize the information and to think more critically about it. This activity will deepen the understanding students have about the concepts within a unit. It will appeal to most learners because the element of choice (an important principle in differentiated classrooms) empowers them to choose a preferred way to express what they know.

Step-by-Step

1. Select activities for students to choose from and compile them on a student handout. See page 33 for a list of suggested activities. You'll find preprinted reproducibles for social studies, science, and language arts on the CD, or you may create your own using the template on the CD.

2. Write a topic you've been studying on the board, such as immigration, biomes, or fairy tales.

3. Ask students to generate terms related to the topic and record them on the blackboard or on an overhead transparency. Or have students record their own lists on the handout you provide (see pages 34–36).

4. Have students choose from among the Fact-Storming choice activities that you provide to show their understanding about the statement or topic.

Allow students to work alone, with a partner, or in a small group. *Remind them to reference as many terms as possible from the list that has been generated.* Students may record their work on paper, or you can supply a transparency and pen for each group so they can share on the overhead later.

5. After students have worked for about 15–20 minutes on their task, bring the whole class back together for sharing. In this way, all students will benefit from reviewing and synthesizing the material from different perspectives.

6. Finally, you might assign a second choice activity for homework. Students should select a different activity from their first activity. Serving as an individual formative assessment, this second writing opportunity will allow students to process information even more deeply, and will further enhance their learning.

TechConnect

VoiceThread, a finalist in the 2008 Webware 100 Awards, provides online space for images and student recordings to be posted. VoiceThread is a place to hold many descriptions of any image.

To use VoiceThread with the FactStorming assessment strategy, show students a series of photos related to a topic they have been studying. Form small groups and allow each group to choose one way (see the FactStorming Choice Activities on page 33) to make sense of the images. Allow students to work together to analyze the images and put together a summary statement about the information. Then, instruct the "reporter" for each group to record the group's response using a microphone (or by typing text, if a microphone is unavailable).

For more info: http://www.voicethread.com

FactStorming Choice Activities

To make sense of the topic, choose from the following activities:

For Social Studies

- Create a time line to sequence at least five key events. Provide a caption detailing the significance of each event.
- Categorize all of the terms (details) into groups and provide a label for each group (main idea). Write a brief summary highlighting the main ideas.
- Rank all of the events in order of importance and defend your choices in a written summary.
- Choose at least three events and elaborate by adding details to describe them.
- Choose at least three events, circumstances, factors, beliefs, or ideas whose effects can still be felt today. (Provide specific written evidence of their effects on life today.)
- Choose at least three events, circumstances, factors, beliefs, or ideas and describe their causes or their effects.
- Choose at least three events, circumstances, factors, beliefs, or ideas and compare them to others you have learned about.

For Science

- Choose at least three terms and elaborate by adding details to describe them.
- Choose at least three terms and describe their cause or effect.
- Illustrate at least three terms and write a description of the significance of each.
- Choose at least three terms that are related. Describe the relationship clearly using scientific terminology. Do this for a second group of at least three terms.
- Choose at least three terms and compare them to something else we have studied.

For Language Arts

- Choose one character. Compare and contrast this character with two others in the story (or compare and contrast this character with two members of your group).
- Choose one character and describe how this character changes over time. Include at least _____ ways this character changes and why these changes occur.
- Choose at least three themes and give evidence from the story of these themes in action.
- Sequence at least five events from the story and discuss how they each affected the main character.
- Choose at least three actions the main character takes and discuss the character's motivation. (Why does he/she take each action?)

FactStorming | Social Studies

Name _____ Date _____

_____

[blank box]

Using as many terms and references as you can from the list you have created, choose one of the activities below to show your understanding of the statement or topic.

■ **Create a time line** to sequence at least five key events. Provide a caption detailing the significance of each event.

■ **Categorize all of the terms** (details) into groups and provide a label for each group (main idea). Write a brief summary using the terms.

■ **Rank all of the events** in order of importance and defend your choices in a written summary.

■ **Choose at least three events** and elaborate by adding details to describe them.

■ **Choose at least three events, circumstances, factors, beliefs, or ideas** whose effects can still be felt today. (Provide specific written evidence of their effects on life today.)

■ **Choose at least three events, circumstances, factors, beliefs, or ideas** and describe their causes or their effects.

■ **Choose at least three events, circumstances, factors, beliefs, or ideas** and compare them to others you have learned about.

FactStorming | Science

Name _____ Date _____

Statement or Topic _____

_____

(blank box)

Using as many terms and references as you can from the list you have created, choose one of the activities below to show your understanding of the statement or topic.

- **Categorize all of the terms** (details) into groups and provide a label for each group (main idea) Create a graphic organizer to display your organization.

- **Choose several terms** and use them to write a brief summary highlighting the main ideas.

- **Choose at least three terms** and describe their cause or their effect.

- **Choose at least three terms and elaborate** by adding details to describe each one.

- **Illustrate at least three terms** and write a description of the significance of each.

- **Choose at least three terms that are related**. Describe the relationship clearly using scientific terminology. Do this for a second group of at least three terms.

- **Choose at least three terms** and compare each one to something else we have studied.

FactStorming | English Language Arts

Name _____ Date _____

_____

Using as many terms and references as you can from the list you have created, choose one of the activities below to show your understanding of the statement or the reading.

■ **Choose one character. Compare and contrast** this character with two others in the story (or, compare and contrast this character with two members of your group).

■ **Choose one character** and describe how this character **changes over time** in at least two ways. Explain why these changes occur.

■ **Choose at least three themes** and give evidence from the story of these themes in action.

■ **Sequence at least five events** from the story and discuss how they each affected the main character.

■ **Illustrate at least three symbols** from the story and write a description of the significance of each.

■ **Choose at least three actions the main character took** and discuss the character's motivation (Why did he/she take each action?)

Section 2

■ ■ ■ ■ ■ ■ ■ ■ ■ ■ ■ ■ ■ ■ ■ ■

Lists, Charts, and Graphic Organizers

The formative assessment strategies that follow include student-made lists, charts, and other graphic organizers. Focusing on logical-mathematical intelligence, the activities ask students to think about their own learning and to reorganize information by generating their own graphic organizers.

Simply photocopying a graphic organizer and requiring that students fill it out will not ensure deep learning or provide an authentic assessment opportunity (Fisher & Frey, 2007). Instead, we need to provide opportunities for students to create their own organizers. Greg Freeman, in David Hyerle's book *A Field Guide to Using Visual Tools* (2000), explains how these graphic organizers help students to "scan the information, make sense of it, and see the pattern that the teacher is helping them connect." These student-created graphic organizers provide insight into students' comprehension and demonstrate personal understanding and reasoning, rather than just literal recall (Irwin-DeVitis & Pease, 1995).

Following are five strategies that invite students to reflect on their learning experiences by listing what they consider most important, by grouping and categorizing terms, by showing connections among concepts, and by generating their own graphic organizers.

My Top Ten List

My Top Ten List is an engaging way for students to review their notes and texts to determine the most important ideas and concepts learned in a unit of study. My Top Ten List will represent essential concepts about a particular topic that students must know and understand to be conversant about the topic. As you help them to develop these lists, you will also be guiding them in learning the critical concept of distinguishing between main ideas and details.

Step-by-Step

1. Provide students a template of My Top Ten List (see page 40 as well as variations on the CD for Math, Science, Social Studies, and English Language Arts).

2. Model the creation of a My Top Ten List using a topic listed under Applications or one of your own choosing. Ask all students to contribute their ideas. As they do so, place their responses on the board under one of the following columns: "main ideas" and "details." (Discuss the difference between a main idea—the principal ideas—and a detail—the specific facts about a main idea.)

3. After students have exhausted their responses, let partners narrow the list down to the top ten.

4. Share as a whole class and try to come to some consensus about the main ideas. Help students recognize what is most significant about this unit of study.

5. Let students work with a partner to develop the next few lists that you assign. Allow them to use their notes and texts when compiling lists the first few times. After students come to know what a "quality response" looks like, one that provides main ideas, essential understandings, and key concepts rather than less important details, you can have students work on this activity individually.

6. Use this strategy periodically, every other week or so, so that students learn to focus on what is important. By using it frequently, students will come to anticipate and think about what they will include in their next My Top Ten List. They may even ask you to assign this task!

Applications

USING MY TOP TEN LIST ACROSS THE CURRICULUM

This strategy can be used to synthesize learning in any subject area. You can choose fro m among the following ideas or create your own.

ENGLISH LANGUAGE ARTS: MY TOP TEN LIST

about a character: attributes, quotes, what others say about the character, what others think about the character, what actions the character takes, what conflicts the character has, how the character changes over time

SOCIAL STUDIES: MY TOP TEN LIST

about a famous historical figure: the place or time period in which the person lived, his or her background or position, the person's accomplishments and his/her impact on society, the person's attributes, obstacles the person may have overcome

SOCIAL STUDIES: MY TOP TEN LIST

about an event: a description of what it is or was, the place and time period in which it occurred, its purpose, its causes and effects, its significance, who was involved with it

MATH OR SCIENCE: MY TOP TEN LIST

about a math or science concept: its definition, attributes, characteristics, and examples; what category it belongs to; how it works; steps involved in it; tips and hints to help remember it; when we might use it in real life; why it's important to know about

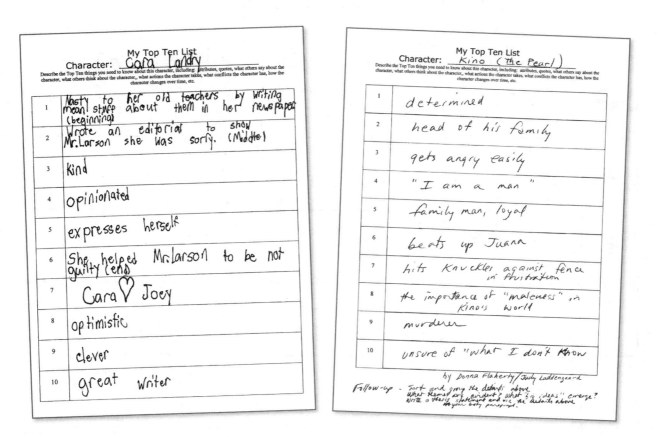

My Top Ten List

Character: Cara Landry

Describe the Top Ten things you need to know about this character, including: attributes, quotes, what others say about the character, what others think about the character, what actions the character takes, what conflicts the character has, how the character changes over time, etc.

1	Nasty to her old teachers by writing mean stuff about them in her newspaper (beginning)
2	Wrote an editorial to show Mr. Larson she was sorry. (Middle)
3	kind
4	opinionated
5	expresses herself
6	She helped Mr. Larson to be not guilty (end)
7	Cara ♥ Joey
8	optimistic
9	clever
10	great writer

My Top Ten List

Character: Kino (The Pearl)

Describe the Top Ten things you need to know about this character, including: attributes, quotes, what others say about the character, what others think about the character, what actions the character takes, what conflicts the character has, how the character changes over time, etc.

1	determined
2	head of his family
3	gets angry easily
4	"I am a man"
5	family man, loyal
6	beats up Juana
7	hits knuckles against fence in frustration
8	the importance of "maleness" in Kino's world
9	murderer
10	unsure of "what I don't know

by Donna Flaherty / Judy Laddengaard

Follow-up - Sort and group the details above
What themes are evident? what "big ideas" emerge?
Write a thesis statement and use the details above
in your body paragraph.

These fifth and eighth grade students use My Top Ten List to sort what they know about the main characters in the novels they have read. Using the details listed, the second student prepares to write a thesis statement and paragraph showing his understanding of the themes that have emerged through this activity. (This template is available on the CD.)

Tips for Tiering!

In addition to the ideas on page 9, consider the following.

To support struggling learners: Provide students a list of statements. Let them use their notes to answer whether each statement is true or false. If the statement is false, tell them to make it true. (For example: *The urban community has wide-open spaces, farms, small villages, and some isolated houses. False. The rural community has wide-open spaces, farms, small villages, and some isolated houses.*)

Continue to allow students to work with peers and/or consult their texts and notes as they develop their lists.

To challenge advanced learners: Challenge these students by asking them to prioritize their My Top Ten List from least important to most important (number 10 being the least important and number 1 being the most important).

Make classroom posters of some of your My Top Ten Lists to help activate prior knowledge for new units of study and to remind students of all that they've learned throughout the year. Make frequent references to the posters and note connections to help students integrate their understandings and come to see all learning as interwoven. A worthy teaching goal would be to help students make their own references and connections during class discussions and written assignments from the My Top Ten List posters. Provide bonus points to students who refer to the posters in their conversation or writing.

My Top Ten Lists will become a favorite for some students. Offer it as one option for students to choose on "Choice Homework Night" a once-a-week or biweekly opportunity for students to choose from a menu of homework choices carefully modeled over time. (See Dodge [2005] for additional ideas about how to use Choice Homework Night to provide homework options that appeal to students with diverse interests and strengths.)

My Top Ten List

Name _____ Date _____

Topic _____

1	
2	
3	
4	
5	
6	
7	
8	
9	
10	

Matrix

Charts and tables help us organize our thinking. As students grapple to understand the great deal of information that comes their way, graphic organizers such as charts, tables, webs, and flow maps can help them see visual patterns and relationships. When studying a unit that has several ideas, people, principles, or other items to compare, the Matrix strategy can help students make sense of the information.

Like a Venn diagram, the Matrix is a visual tool that helps students make comparisons among items. Unlike a Venn diagram, however, the Matrix can be used to compare and contrast many items at once. Be sure to provide multiple opportunities for designing and using this tool with your students before you use it as an independent assessment tool.

Topic: U.S. Documents   Matrix

Items to be Compared/Categories:

Characteristics/ Features:	#1 Mayflower Compact	#2 Declaration of Independence	#3 US Constitution	#4 Bill of Rights
Year	1620	1776	1787	1791
Created By	Pilgrims	Founders like Thomas Jefferson	state representatives	Congress (approved)
Where?	Plymouth, Mass.	Philadelphia, PA	Philadelphia, PA	New York City, NY
What is it?	plan for government	an explanation for why colonists should be independent	"framework"/plan for government	First 10 amendments of Constitution
Purpose	live under common government	government should serve people and protect their rights	spell out the exact powers of the federal government and relationship with state government	to protect individual rights from government abuse
Important Facts or Quotes	beginning of self-government in America	"all men created equal" "life, liberty and the pursuit of happiness"	3 separate branches - checks and balances	freedom of speech, press and religion

Social Studies students use the Matrix to compare and contrast several U.S. documents. (This template is available on the CD.)

Step-by-Step

1. Duplicate and distribute the Matrix template (page 43).

2. Model for students how you would fill out the chart as you guide them in a rich discussion in review of a topic (comparing characters, states of matter, types of landforms, characteristics of communities/regions/biomes, etc.).

3. Have students fill in a chart of their own as you model and complete yours.

4. Provide students the language of compare-contrast (see box page 42) so that they can speak and communicate clearly about the differences and similarities of the items being discussed.

5. As a follow-up, have students write a compare-contrast essay using at least five of the terms listed on page 42.

6. After the next day's reading or lesson, allow partners to work together to complete a Matrix template to organize and compare the information.

7. Once students are comfortable and confident in the use of this strategy to organize and compare information, assign independent tasks in which they do so.

D emonstrate to students how they can de-sign tables with varying rows and columns, depending upon the number of items and the number of characteristics being compared.

Ultimately, the goal for using the Matrix is for students to be able to create them on their own (instead of filling in a template) so they can use them for independent study or research. At first, you can provide templates for students to complete during a lesson. Later, you can ask students to create their own charts after a homework reading assignment. You can also ask students to reorganize information from their class notes by designing their own chart to serve as a study guide.

Charts like the Matrix can be used to help students in decision making (McKenzie, 1997). Model how you might use a matrix to evaluate data and draw conclusions about it. For example:

Which snacks should be placed in the vending machine at school?			
	Fats	Calories	Sodium
Trail Mix			
Potato Chips			
Pretzels			

Here are some other ways to use the Matrix.

IN ENGLISH LANGUAGE ARTS, TO COMPARE:

- different genres
- characters
- stories in an author study

IN SOCIAL STUDIES, TO COMPARE:

- time periods, civilizations
- countries, states, or regions
- political/historical figures or groups

IN SCIENCE, TO COMPARE:

- human systems
- ecosystems
- weather and climate

IN MATH, TO COMPARE:

- problem-solving strategies
- geometric shapes
- types of graphs

I n addition to the ideas on page 9, consider the following.

To support struggling learners: Continue to provide students the characteristics by which to compare the items.

Provide a partially completed chart.

To challenge advanced learners: Ask students to make comparisons by choosing their own characteristics.

Ask students to compare items to others that are not in this unit of study—for example, those learned previously, those experienced in their own life, or those that exist in society.

The Language of *Compare and Contrast*

▼

T he Matrix organizes information for compare-and-contrast analyses. Reinforce this purpose by creating a classroom poster of the transition words used to compare and contrast; see below. Encourage students to use these words in order to communicate more logically and coherently. Point out to students when a particular word or phrase from the list might help their speech or writing become more precise.

Both	Similar to
In comparison	Much as
Each	In the same way
However	And
Similarly	Also
Instead	On the contrary
In common	Same
In contrast	But
One difference	Different
Neither	Although
Even though	Whereas

Matrix

Name _____ Date _____

Characteristics / Features:	Items to be Compared/Categories		
	#1	#2	#3

Noting What I've Learned

Noting What I've Learned is a simple note-taking strategy that can be used in all grade levels and across the curriculum. Adapted from my favorite new note-taking strategy, Column Note Taking, it utilizes the best element of this note-taking system popularized at Cornell University (Pauk, 2000): two columns, one for main ideas and another for details. Keeping this basic format, I've added boxes so students can provide drawings and other nonlinguistic representations of the information, and I've enumerated the details to make outlining simple and inviting for beginning note takers (Dodge, 1994). This format of note taking with both pictures and words is inviting to learners who are spatial and enjoy illustrating their ideas.

Used with struggling students or students new to note taking, Noting What I've Learned provides an introduction to a critical skill that students must master to be successful in school. Since students' organizational skills and ability to function independently vary greatly in a mixed-readiness classroom, you need to begin note-taking instruction with a very basic note-taking format and then offer alternative strategies and less structured formats when students seem ready (Dodge, 2005).

Step-by-Step

1. Provide students with a template of Noting What I've Learned to accompany a reading assignment (page 46).

2. If this is the first time your students are using this outline, provide them the Main Ideas, Questions, or Key Words for each of the boxes. (Each box should reflect one section of the reading.)

3. Read aloud one section from your textbook or other nonfiction text, and then pause. Give students two to three minutes to list details (facts, data, examples, evidence, and so on) supporting the main idea or to answer the question that is written in the box.

4. To provide students additional support with this note-taking instruction, you might allow partners first to talk for one minute to gather ideas before writing individually.

5. Have students share ideas as a whole class, so that all students can learn from one another.

6. Read the next textbook section aloud. Follow steps 4 and 5. Repeat until section is completed.

7. Show students how to use Noting What I've Learned as an effective study tool by folding the right side of the page over to meet the right side of the boxes. Students can then study by asking themselves questions and trying to answer them aloud without looking at the details underneath the folded paper. (See the sample on page 45.)

8. Change to a different activity for the rest of your lesson. You will want to practice this reading and note taking/sharing at least once a week for part of the class period. Over time, students will build their note-taking skills and will be able to read and take notes more independently.

Applications

This strategy can be used for listening comprehension, as well. As part of your lesson, you might give a PowerPoint presentation, show a video, or play a podcast (digital media files downloaded off the Internet). Every few minutes, stop for students to record what they have heard on their Noting What I've Learned organizer.

Once students have been given direct and guided instruction, as well as paired practice, they will be ready to use the Noting What I've Learned template on their own for homework. Frequent practice with this strategy will make better note takers of your students.

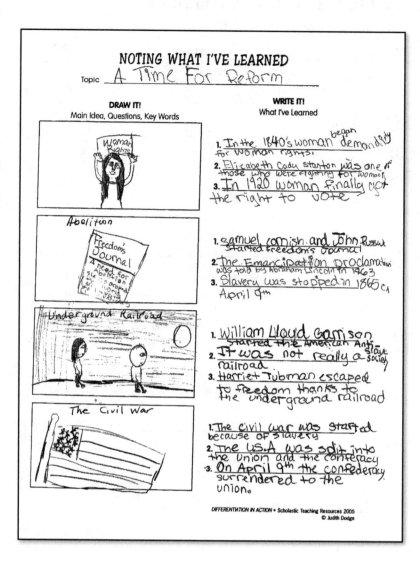

NOTING WHAT I'VE LEARNED

Topic _A Time For Reform_

DRAW IT!
Main Idea, Questions, Key Words

WRITE IT!
What I've Learned

Woman Rights

1. In the 1840's woman began demanding for woman rights.
2. Elizabeth Cady stanton was one of those who were fighting for woman.
3. In 1920 woman finally got the right to vote

Abolition
Freedom's Journal
A need for Abolition around the world

1. samuel cornish and John Russel started freedom's Journal
2. The Emancipation proclamation was told by Abraham Lincoln in 1863
3. Slavery was stopped in 1865 CA April 9th

Underground Railroad

1. William Lloyd Garrison started the American Anti-slave society
2. It was not really a railroad.
3. Harriet Tubman escaped to freedom thanks to the underground railroad

The Civil War

1. The Civil war was started because of slavery
2. The U.S.A was split into the Union and the conferacy
3. On April 9th the confederacy surrendered to the union.

DIFFERENTIATION IN ACTION ● Scholastic Teaching Resources 2005
© Judith Dodge

Students use the Noting What I've Learned outline to organize their notes for Social Studies. (This template is available on the CD.)

TechConnect ➤

Have groups of students plan PowerPoint presentations using the Noting What I've Learned graphic organizer as their prewriting/organizational tool. During presentations, have other students listen and record their own notes on a blank Noting What I've Learned outline.

Tips for Tiering!

In addition to the ideas on page 9, consider the following.

To support struggling learners: Continue to provide the main ideas, questions, or key words for these students as long as needed.

Provide the page number, paragraph, or section where students will find the details they will need.

Highlight sections of the text to help English language learners focus on comprehending a smaller amount of text.

To challenge advanced learners: Encourage advanced note takers to take notes in whatever format works best for them.

Noting What I've Learned

Name _____ Date _____

Topic _____

Draw It! Main Ideas, Questions, Key Words	**Write It!** What I've Learned

Draw It!
Main Ideas, Questions, Key Words

Write It!
What I've Learned

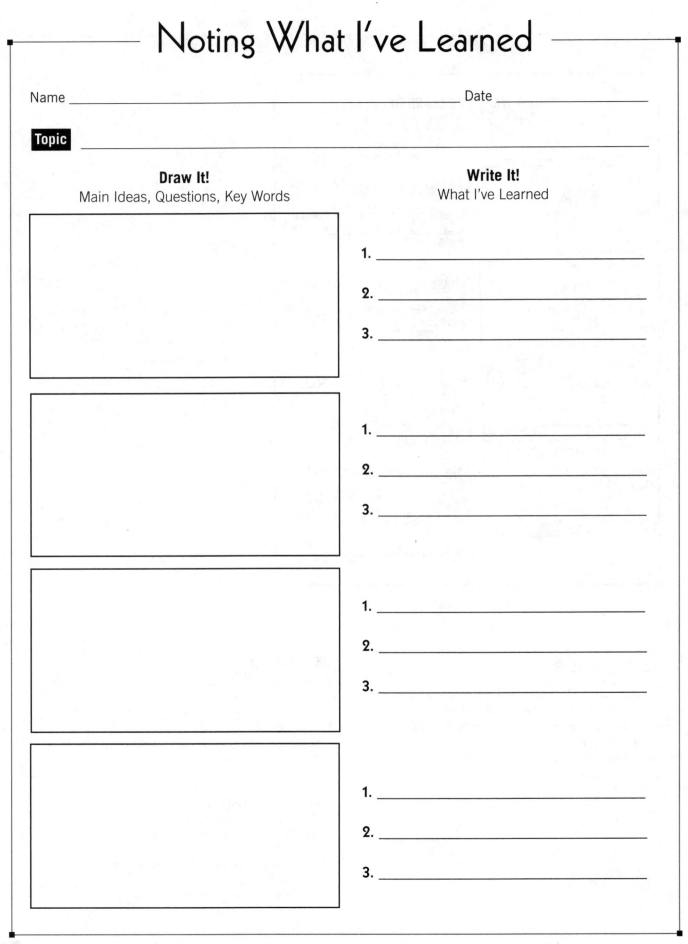

1. _____

2. _____

3. _____

1. _____

2. _____

3. _____

1. _____

2. _____

3. _____

1. _____

2. _____

3. _____

List-Group-Label

List-Group-Label (Taba, 1967) is a strategy that helps students make sense of information and develop their vocabulary. It requires students to list and sort terms to activate prior knowledge or review concepts after a unit of study. Used as a formative assessment, List-Group-Label measures student understanding of a topic or concept.

In a "closed" sort, the teacher provides the categories, or labels, for organizing the terms related to the topic. Students group the terms according to the teacher's suggested labels. In an "open" sort, students use their critical-thinking skills to create their own labels for sorting and grouping the terms.

Since the brain is a category seeker, List-Group-Label is a brain-friendly activity. It helps students retain information more easily. It also raises the level of thinking because it asks that students make sense of the facts, data, and terms by noting relationships. Students completing an open sort will find very different ways to group the terms and make sense of the information. There is no "right" way to sort the terms, as long as the students can explain the grouping by making an accurate connection. The conversation and discussion that are part of this exercise are usually rich with content vocabulary and generally lead to meaning making at critical levels of thinking.

As List-Group-Label can be designed as an open-ended strategy, it addresses the needs of students of all readiness levels. Struggling and grade-level students will see the more obvious connections; advanced learners will make broader connections, tying information they are learning now to ideas from other disciplines and to topics previously covered.

Step-by-Step

1. Choose a topic, concept, or theme that you have been studying.

2. Write it on the board or an overhead transparency.

3. Ask students to generate as many terms as they can that relate to the topic, concept, or theme. You can guide this activity with questions to evoke specific vocabulary. (*What were the causes of the Revolutionary War? How did the colonists respond?*) Record between 25 and 30 terms.

4. Provide categories for the students to complete a closed sort (for example: *British actions against the Colonists, Colonists' reactions, Battles, Spies*) Ask partners to group the terms according to each label.

5. Ask several pairs of students to share the terms they have placed under each label and to explain the connections they have made—for example: *These terms all relate to the causes of the American Revolution. They are all actions taken by the King of England against the colonists.*

6. Alternatively, complete steps 1–3 and then have students engage in an open sort, organizing the terms in their own way and coming up with their own labels.

Applications

As a follow-up, you can have students write a summary of the topic, using as many main ideas (categories) and details (terms) as they can in their writing. This writing exercise is good practice for an essay that might come later as a summative assessment.

Terms can be listed on a handout and students can be given a graphic organizer to help them sort the information. Terms can also be written on flash cards, making grouping and regrouping an easier task for students. Tactile-kinesthetic learners will appreciate the opportunity to move the cards around from group to group to make sense of the terms.

You can photocopy a set of terms in boxes or students can fill in boxes on their own blank template as you develop a class-generated list of terms. Then, each student can cut apart the boxes, creating his or her own set of flash cards. The template on page 49 will make it easy for you to create materials for either an open sort or a closed sort.

Tips for Tiering!

In addition to the ideas on page 9, consider the following.

To support struggling learners: Provide the terms on flash cards so they can be manipulated and moved around easily into different groups.

For second-language learners or students who struggle with vocabulary, provide the entire list of terms (or cards) in random order, as well as a list of categories, so they will be engaged in a matching activity.

Provide one example of a label/category and a group of terms; ask that they find other groups and provide labels/categories.

Provide students with several groups of words, already sorted; ask them to label the groups.

To challenge advanced learners: Have these students work together to take the topic and generate their own list of terms. Then, have them group and label all of the terms.

Encourage these students to extend their thinking by allowing them to work with the terms and categories on a large sheet of paper with markers. Have them create a concept map or semantic map, showing categories, as well as hierarchical relationships (degree of importance) among the terms. Explain that they can use large boxes or circles to indicate that an idea has a greater degree of importance than one in a small box or circle. Provide students with a list of "linking terms" (see Web Wind-Up page 51) to help them show deeper, more complex understanding and multiple relationships.

List-Group-Label

- Create a closed or open sort for a List-Group-Label activity.
- List terms that are related to the topic in the boxes below, copy and distribute to students.

Web Wind-Up

The Web Wind-Up is a thought-provoking summarization tool that uses a web to engage students in active learning. Because there is no one way for students to design this graphic organizer, it honors the individual learner in a differentiated classroom and fosters creativity. It encourages critical thinking rather than rote learning because it stresses recognizing concepts and noting relationships among ideas.

Before beginning a new topic of study, assess learners by asking them to demonstrate on a web what they already know about the topic. After studying the material in class, students can return to this web and add information in a different color, creating a "wind-up," or summary web, incorporating what they have learned. Alternatively, they can create an entirely new summary web illustrating what they have come to know and understand. (See examples on page 51 that illustrate a pre-assessment web and a Web Wind-Up on the topic of digestion.)

Step-by-Step

1. Introduce the web graphic organizer by describing its specific purpose: to organize information about a topic or concept with all its details, definitions, attributes, characteristics, and examples visually displayed.

2. Choose a topic or concept that you have been studying and write its name in a circle in the center of a piece of chart paper or on the board. Have students do the same on a sheet of paper. Then have partners work together to brainstorm everything they can that relates to the topic and write their ideas on lines coming off the circle (see sample on page 51).

3. Once students are comfortable and confident using the web with familiar material, you can assign them to use it with new information.

4. Be sure to emphasize the language of "addition" when working with this strategy, as it will reinforce the purpose for using this particular organizer. You might create a classroom poster of "addition words" such as: *first, second, third, and, in addition, also, for instance, for example, to illustrate, besides, furthermore, another,* and *finally.* When students use appropriate addition words in describing a topic with its details and examples, they will communicate more precisely about the topic You'll find a more complete list of transition words in the Appendix, page 94.

Applications

A Web Wind-Up can be a frequent tool for summarizing either a class lesson or an assigned reading. Include it as a "Choice Homework Night"

Web Wind-Ups can also be done in small groups. Give each group a large piece of paper (18" x 24") or a large dry-erase board to demonstrate their understanding of the material covered in that day's (or the previous day's) lesson. Each group should be assigned a recorder, a timer/leader, an illustrator, and a presenter. Groups can present their summaries to one another, or students can take a "gallery walk" to view how different groups have organized the information.

Upon completing the presentations or returning to their seats from the gallery walk, students can write a summary as an individual formative assessment of what they know and understand up to this point.

Topic: Digestion of Food

Pre-Assessment "What I Know About Digestion"

(Digestion web with branches:)
- ① I chew my food
- ② Food travels thru my esophagus to my stomach → small intestines → large intestines
- ③ Food breaks down
- ④ My body uses the nutrients

Post-Assessment: Web Wind-Up (A summary Web) "What I've Learned About Digestion"

(Digestion summary web with branches:)
- ① Food in my mouth — mechanical digestion (teeth, break food into smaller parts); chemical digestion (saliva-moistens, ptyalin-enzyme, chemical reactions)
- ② Esophagus — mucos, peristalsis
- ③ Stomach — enzyme pepsin, hydrochloric acid, mucos-protect stomach, chemical digestion, mechanical digestion, peristalsis
- ④ Small Intestine — most digestion here; Liver + Pancreas - gall bladder help; bile - pancreatic juices; Villi - inner lining of sm. intestine that absorbs food into blood vessel, send nutrients → rest of body
- Large Intestine — undigested food form solid waste - feces → rectum

This science teachers uses a web to pre-assess learners before she begins her unit on digestion. After the unit, students use a Web Wind-up to show what they have learned.

TechConnect ▶

Using software programs like Kidspiration or Inspiration, younger students can create graphic organizers with circles, arrows, spokes, and graphic images, as well as words.

A free web tool for mind mapping, called Mind-meister, is better for older students, as it uses only text. However, the exciting part of this online tool is that it allows any number of students to work together simultaneously to create the graphic organizer. For more info: www.mindmeister.com.

Tips for Tiering!

In addition to the ideas on page 9, consider the following.

To support struggling learners: Continue to provide the main ideas, questions, or key words as needed.

Change the "wheel and spokes" to a box with horizontal lines for students who find the spatial orientation of a web to be visually confusing.

Topic: _____

To challenge advanced learners: Provide these students with "linking terms" to write in color on their webs so that they can note relationships, hierarchy, and changes, as well as the details, attributes, and examples. Encourage them to use words such as:

is /are	contains	therefore
is like/is unlike	is an example of	because
is the same as	another example	determines
is different from	is	by
takes place in	is caused by	symbolizes
during	causes	becomes
because	produces	is made of
is changed by	consists of	is found in
uses	results in	takes place
can be	equals	is changed
represents	is a result of	leads/leads to
involves	as a result	has/have

This additional language will allow students to expand, build, and reflect upon the information in a more complex and sophisticated way.

Encourage these students to draw arrows, boxes, circles, and lines to indicate relationships among the ideas.

Section 3

Visual Representations of Information

The formative assessment strategies that follow ask students to create visual and nonlinguistic representations of information. Marzano, Pickering, and Pollock (2001) describe nonlinguistic representations as "the most underused instructional strategy of all those reviewed" in their book *Classroom Instruction That Works*. This is unfortunate because there is evidence that students who create visual representations of a concept are better able to understand and recall the concept (Ritchie & Karge, 1996, as cited in Fisher & Frey, 2007). Marzano et al. suggest that there are a variety of activities that help students produce nonlinguistic representations (including creating graphic representations, making physical models, generating mental pictures, drawing pictures and pictographs, and engaging in kinesthetic activity). Nonlinguistic representations help students to elaborate, adding to their knowledge. By allowing students to draw, we enhance their understanding of content, and the effects on achievement are strong (Marzano et al., 2001). Providing this type of formative assessment and elaboration increases the likelihood of retention of information later on. Following are seven strategies that invite students to generate visual representations to show their understanding.

Picture Note Making

The Picture Note Making strategy makes sense for our diverse learners. It is both active and motivating, and it appeals to students who have spatial learning preferences. Additionally, it supports the research that suggests ideas are stored in our brain both verbally and in nonverbal image forms (Paivio, 1986).

Although not all learners find visualizing helpful in their learning, there are many who would not have access to the flow of ideas if it were not for the concrete images they can see (McLaughlin & Vogt, 2000). Visualization activities like Picture Note Making provide new opportunities for students to communicate about their learning, which is critical to the social construction of meaning.

Students are given a Picture Note Making template (see page 55) and asked to write three important ideas that they have learned. On the left side of the page they are asked to visualize and then draw a picture to help them remember as much as possible about the topic or concept, including big ideas as well as details. (See example below.)

The pictures can be shared and discussed in pairs or small groups. The conversation about the topic or concept is usually rich in detail because of the variety of illustrations. The images help visual learners retain the information better than simply discussing the concept orally.

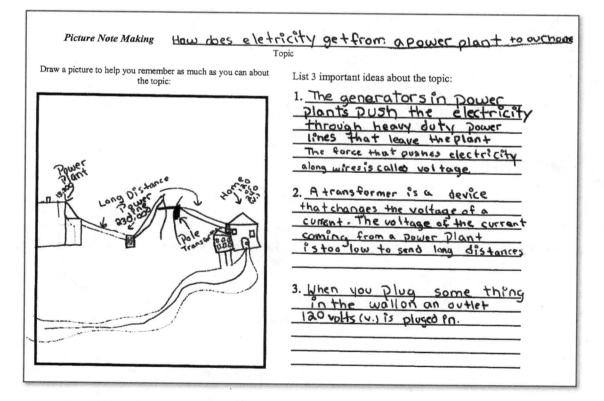

Picture Note Making helps these students make sense of what they've learned in a unit on electricity. Using both linguistic and non-linguistic representations ensures better retention. (This template is available on the CD.)

Step-by-Step

1. After a learning experience (a class discussion, demonstration, reading assignment, research activity, and so on), have students reflect and write about three key understandings ("big ideas") that they have learned about on the Picture Note Making handout.

2. After the writing is complete, allow an additional few minutes for students to sketch images related to the big ideas. (If time is short, you can ask students to finish the drawings at home and hand in the paper the following day.)

3. Collect the papers to assess student learning about the topic or concept. Provide brief comments to students as feedback.

4. Have students engage in a strategy called Sketch to Stretch (Short, Harste, & Burke, 1996), in which they use their pictures to share in small groups. As each student in the group shows his or her Picture Note Making illustration, group members verbally describe what they see and interpret the drawing for themselves. Finally, the writer-artist elaborates and gives his or her own interpretation of the images.

Applications

If you use Picture Note Making several times throughout a particular unit of study, you can have students collate their pages afterwards and put them together to create a book on the topic.

Some teachers I have worked with use Picture Note Making as a follow-up to school-wide assembly programs, a visit from an author, or a field trip.

Other teachers use this strategy as a follow-up to a video or their own PowerPoint presentations to assess what their students have learned.

TechConnect ➤

Have students use Kid Pix software or the free paint tool that comes with Windows to illustrate their understanding in a large box. Students can then give three facts, understandings, or conclusions about the image.

Tips for Tiering!

In addition to the ideas on page 9, consider the following.

To support struggling learners: Suggest that students list any details they can remember (rather than asking them to record the big ideas).

Provide a list of big ideas from which students can choose or from which students can choose one to elaborate upon.

Supply students with pictures to help spark their memories and make the writing flow more easily.

To challenge advanced learners: Ask students to use Picture Note Making to create a "how-to" booklet for other students to read and use (How to Be a Good Friend, How to Deal With a Bully, How to Keep Your Teeth Healthy, How to Recycle in Your Home, How to Solve Math Word Problems).

Picture Note Making

Name _____

Date _____

Topic _____

Draw a picture to help you remember as much as you can about the topic:

List three important ideas about the topic:

1. _____

2. _____

3. _____

QuickWrite/QuickDraw

QuickWrite/QuickDraw is an assessment tool that invites learners to explain their thinking through both writing and drawing. Because this assessment includes both linguistic (left-brain) and nonlinguistic (right-brain) representations, it offers teachers a view into the thinking of learners who might have a preference for one mode of thinking over the other. Marzano et al. advise us that the more we use both systems of representation, linguistic and nonlinguistic, the better we are able to think about and recall knowledge (2001).

On the right side of the page, students write as they analyze information and break it down to show their understanding. As students engage in this "quickwriting," they are able to develop their ideas, reflect on what they know about a topic, and make connections (Tompkins, 1998). The writing side of the assessment engages learners in the process of *elaborative rehearsal*, which is necessary to increase the meaning of semantic information, as well as the likelihood of its retention (Wolfe, 2001). On the left side of the page, students draw symbols or images to synthesize what they know and to show relationships among the information. I find most students enjoy completing this assessment because there is a drawing component to it. The complete QuickWrite/QuickDraw serves as a good study tool later on for students with its memorable images and brief explanations.

Step-by-Step

1. Duplicate the QuickWrite/QuickDraw template on page 58; give one to each student.

2. Allow students to write and draw for between five and ten minutes to show their understanding of a particular concept you have identified. (It is interesting to note whether students write or draw first, as this is probably an indication of their preferred mode of expression. You can keep this in mind when, in the future, you're deciding which assessment strategies to offer students.)

3. Allow students to share their QuickWrite/QuickDraw assessments with one another in small groups as you circulate to listen in on the conversations. Encourage them to add to their own papers after listening to the ideas of their classmates (Tompkins, 1998). Ask them to include this additional information in another color, so they can see the process of their learning and the value of sharing ideas.

4. Collect this completed QuickWrite/QuickDraw and make notes about any misunderstandings or gaps in student understanding. Form a needs-based group to follow up the next day, if necessary.

Tips for Tiering!

In addition to the ideas on page 9, consider the following.

To support struggling learners: Provide written steps or explanations and ask that students create an illustration to represent the information nonlinguistically.

Provide the illustrations and ask that students describe them in words.

Allow two students to work together on a QuickWrite/QuickDraw, with one student writing and the other illustrating.

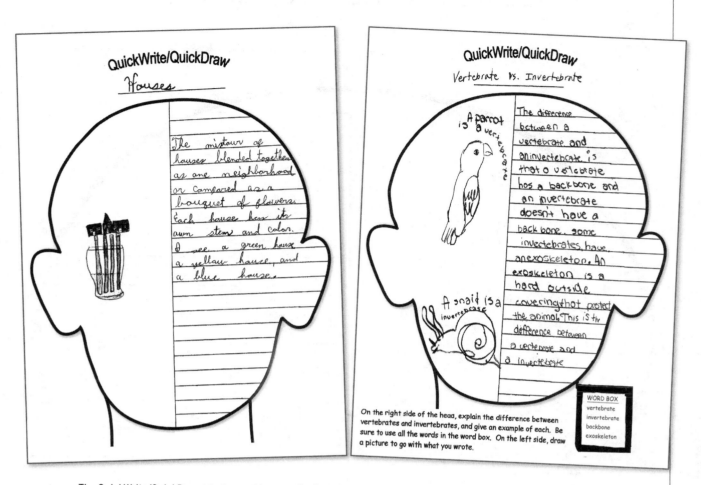

QuickWrite/QuickDraw
Houses

The mixture of houses blended together as one neighborhood or compared as a bouquet of flowers. Each house has its own stem and color. I see a green house a yellow house, and a blue house.

QuickWrite/QuickDraw
Vertebrate vs. Invertebrate

A parrot is a vertebrate

A snail is a invertebrate

The difference between a vertebrate and an invertebrate, is that a vertebrate has a backbone and an invertebrate doesn't have a back bone. Some invertebrates have an exoskeleton. An exoskeleton is a hard outside covering that protect the animal. This is the difference between a vertebrate and a invertebrate

On the right side of the head, explain the difference between vertebrates and invertebrates, and give an example of each. Be sure to use all the words in the word box. On the left side, draw a picture to go with what you wrote.

WORD BOX
vertebrate
invertebrate
backbone
exoskeleton

The QuickWrite/QuickDraw strategy addresses the fact that our brain is a "dual-processor." As the student on the left listens to a poem that his teacher reads aloud, he draws the images that he sees in his mind and, afterwards, explains his understanding in words. The science student on the right is guided by a word box his teacher has provided to help him compare vertebrates and invertebrates by both writing and drawing. (This template is available on the CD.)

Applications

The QuickWrite/QuickDraw is a useful assessment for showing understanding about the following

IN SCIENCE:

- Sequence/steps/cycles/processes
- Scientific principles
- Content-area vocabulary

IN MATH:

- Steps in a process
- Clocks/money/shapes/patterns/ measurement

IN SOCIAL STUDIES:

- Important events/turning points/conflicts
- Elements of civilization
- Highlights of an era
- Content-area vocabulary

IN ENGLISH LANGUAGE ARTS:

- Characters/key figures/attributes
- Setting/conflict/problems and solutions
- Beginning, middle, end
- Symbols/themes

QuickWrite/QuickDraw

Name _____ Date _____

Unit Collage

A Unit Collage is a student-generated, ongoing, visual synthesis of a topic studied in class. It includes on one page a group of eight to ten drawings, symbols, captions, and so forth that capture the essence of a unit of study. Creating individual unit collages allows students to process information more deeply through their own synthesis of ideas, both visual and linguistic. The benefits of completing a Unit Collage are many. Because the collages are fairly open-ended, they appeal to learners of different strengths and intelligences. Along the way, these collages serve as a check for student understanding and an opportunity for informal assessment. These collages will later serve as effective study tools and triggers for student memory. Some students choose to save the collages for years, keeping a visual record of some of the most important ideas, principles, and key concepts that they have studied in a particular class.

This teacher's colorful display of students' Unit Collages about the regions of the United States allows students to reference the information learned in past units as they work to make sense of new units of study. (This template is available on the CD.)

Step-by-Step

1. It is important to model for the class how to create a Unit Collage. If you are not comfortable with illustrating ideas yourself, engage one of your student artists to create the first one with you.

2. Take a poster-size sheet of paper and divide it into at least six boxes. Place the heading, topic, or title of the unit at the top of the page.

3. Throughout the unit, stop after discussing an important concept/subtopic and brainstorm with the entire class how you could illustrate the concept to make it memorable. Together, decide what vocabulary terms, phrases, or quotes should be included in addition to the picture or drawing.

4. Illustrate the particular concept you're working on, adding any important content-specific language that the class has decided is necessary to describe the concept accurately.

5. Continue with the study of the unit, which may take several more days, or even weeks, until its conclusion. Along the way, stop periodically to create a new block when you determine that it would be helpful to increase retention.

6. At the end of the unit, use the class-generated Unit Collage to help review the unit. (You may decide to have more than one poster page, depending upon the complexity of the unit.)

7. Students should now be ready to create their own individual Unit Collages for the next unit.

8. Before you photocopy the reproducible on page 62 for students to use, decide whether you want to run off the copies with subtopics or questions printed in each box. This is usually helpful for younger students or those with weak organizational skills.

9. Stop periodically throughout the unit for students to fill in a box on their collage. Midway through a lesson, brainstorm ideas with the class and then provide five minutes or so for students to individually complete the box as a check for understanding. Or you might give students five minutes at the end of the lesson as closure. Alternatively, you can assign one box for homework and have students share their collage the next day with a partner.

Types of Information/Visuals to Include on a Unit Collage

- Key understandings or concepts
- Formulas
- Principles
- Parts and functions
- Examples
- Pictures
- Symbols
- Themes
- Story elements
- Literary devices
- Quotes
- Tips and hints
- Key figures
- Turning points
- Major contributions
- Legacies
- Important events
- Content vocabulary terms

Tips for Tiering!

In addition to the ideas on page 9, consider the following.

To support struggling learners: Label each box on the unit collage with a key concept, quote, or example to guide students.

To challenge advanced learners: Leave the task more open-ended, allowing these students to determine what is important in the unit and how they should synthesize and record the information.

Have students make a connection that you did not discuss in class between two ideas in this unit, or have students compare something they learned in this unit with something they learned previously. Ask students to write each connection or comparison in one of the boxes on the Unit Collage.

Eliminate this activity completely for this group of learners and substitute a more complex, higher-level task (see ideas for FactStorming on page 32 for more rigorous thinking activities).

Group Unit Collages: While students will enjoy keeping their own individual Unit Collages, periodically place students in heterogeneous groups to complete a Group Unit Collage as a review for an entire unit. Provide a list of key elements that must be included in each of the groups' collages. Allow 20–30 minutes for groups to complete the task using any resources they have (textbook, notebooks, handouts, and so on). During the last few minutes of class, conduct a gallery walk for students to visit all of the posters.

If you are willing to let this activity take a little more time, it can be even more effective. Let student groups present the information on their collages to the rest of the class. Then distribute a practice assessment with short response questions to each student. Allow students to take a "gallery walk," return to their seats, and complete the assessment individually. Permit students to go back to any collage for additional help in completing the assessment. This is, after all, a formative assessment, not a summative assessment. This practice strategy is for learning. The questions will help students continue to process more deeply the information they have been studying.

(On the CD, you will find another version of the Unit Collage.)

TechConnect ▸

To create a digital Unit Collage, students can use PowerPoint to create one slide with seven or eight images. First, students will create a folder and save pictures as they scan them from their own drawings or download them from the Internet. Then, they will create a background for their slide and insert onto the slide each picture that they've saved. Finally, students will insert a text box next to each image for description, summary, or analysis.

A science student uses the Unit Collage to create a visual summary on the topic of Matter.

Unit Collage

Name _____ Date _____

Subtopic/Question:	Subtopic/Question:

Subtopic/Question:	Subtopic/Question:

_____
Topic

Subtopic/Question:	Subtopic/Question:

Subtopic/Question:	Subtopic/Question:

Photo Finish

Photo Finish is a series of snapshot visuals that captures the essence of a topic. Spatial learners will welcome the occasional opportunity to show you what they know through their own illustrations.

In the 1800's we used steamboats and used it for trades

THEN:

In the 1800's the trains were very small and had no brakes

In the 1800's the Erie Canal boats were pulled by mules

In the 1800's they rode on coaches pulled by horses.

NOW:

Photo Finish

Now we go on cruise ships for fun and vacation.

Today trains can be very long and fit many people.

Now many people use the Erie Canal for fishing.

Now we ride cars that run on gasoline.

Through drawing and writing a Photo Finish, this student compares transportation in the 1800s with transportation now. (This template is available on the CD.)

I remember one fourth-grade student who was classified as learning disabled because of his difficulty with writing. I was visiting his class, and they had just finished a unit of study about communities. Knowing his strength was drawing, I asked him to make an illustration to show me his understanding of how the suburban, urban, and rural communities compared to one another. Had I asked him instead to write about those differences, I would have been inaccurate in my assessment of what he understood conceptually. His very detailed sketches showed me his understanding of the different homes, jobs, lifestyles, and physical features found in each type of community. I remember how proud he was as I praised his deep knowledge and understanding. I decided to tell his teacher to work on his writing skills the following day, allowing him to bask in the good feelings he was experiencing during this moment.

1. As always, it is important to model for the class how to complete any new strategy. If you are not comfortable with illustrating ideas yourself, engage one of your student artists to create the first one with you.

2. Copy and distribute the Photo Finish reproducible on page 66. This version has eight boxes for illustration; you'll find alternative versions on the CD, or you may make your own.

3. Throughout the unit, stop after discussing an important concept and brainstorm with the entire class how you could illustrate the concept to make it memorable. Together, decide what vocabulary terms, phrases, or quotes should be recorded in addition to the picture or drawing.

4. Model your thinking about how you choose what key ideas to illustrate and how you will represent them. For example, after a unit on the three branches of government, I begin my modeling like this:

> We have been studying the three branches of government, and I remember that the legislative branch makes the laws about trading, money making, and paying taxes. So, in the first box, I will write "legislative branch" and "laws." Then, in the second snapshot box, I'll sketch outline maps of the

United States and England with arrows indicating their trade. In the third box, I'll draw a picture of several bills ($1, $5, $10, and $20) and write "money making." Finally, I'll draw the dollar symbol with an arrow pointing to the word "government" to show that the legislative branch makes the laws about paying taxes.

5. Continue to model your thinking process as you complete a Photo Finish to show what you know about the executive and judicial branches of government.

6. Once you have guided students in developing meaningful nonlinguistic representations of information, you can give them practice doing this on their own. You might list four key ideas for students and allow them to brainstorm with partners for two or three minutes about which symbols or illustrations they could draw to represent the concepts. Then, give students just a few minutes to complete their individual drawings. (Some students could go on drawing forever, so be sure to advise them that these sketches should be brief and include simple art work, such as stick figures.) If you use a timer and say, "Pencils down!" at a given point, your slowest artists will soon understand that they have to start immediately and keep it simple. If drawing is difficult for some students, encourage them to try, but allow them to write about their understanding instead.

Applications

Give students the Photo Finish template (page 66) to assess their understanding of:

- Major contributions
- Characters/key figures
- Turning points
- Important events
- Examples of … themes/story elements/literary devices/conflicts

- Different groups or categories
- Cause and effect
- Change over time
- Before and after
- Sequence/important events/steps
- Compare and contrast
- Beginning, middle, end

Tips for Tiering!

In addition to the ideas on page 9, consider the following.

To support struggling learners: Provide students with a cause (in writing) and have them illustrate this cause and one effect. Or provide students with four pictures (four causes) and let them illustrate an appropriate effect for each.

Provide students with out-of-sequence sentence strips indicating steps, sequence, or change over time. Have them sequence the ideas and then draw an illustration to represent each of the ideas.

Provide students with several pictures. Have them sort the pictures to compare and contrast concepts. Explain to them that some of the pictures will not be used (this will encourage the students to think more critically than if they were engaged in a simple matching exercise). When they have chosen from among the pictures, let them paste the illustrations onto the Photo Finish template to show the comparisons.

To challenge advanced learners: Ask these students to use Photo Finish to show higher-level thinking by illustrating:

- Cause and effect
- Change over time
- Before and after
- Sequence/steps
- Compare and contrast

Keep in mind that some students will simply be unable to illustrate as a way of showing understanding. A Photo Finish, therefore, is not an effective assessment tool for everyone. When some students do poorly on this activity, it does not imply lack of understanding about concepts, but rather a discomfort with drawing. Since we are not trying to measure artistic skills in the content-area classroom, we should be prepared to provide these students with an alternate assessment strategy that requires writing instead of drawing, or one that provides the pictures for students to describe. Remember, it is important to have a repertoire of assessment tools so that over time you can gather accurate evidence of understanding from your diverse learners.

TechConnect ➤

Using Photo Story (a free download from Microsoft .com), you can have students create a slide show by choosing digital photos and creating a descriptive audio track to run concurrently. If you want to add music, as well as audio, you can pull Photo Story into Movie Maker (it comes free with Windows XP and Vista) and add a music track to the background.

For more info: http://www.microsoft.com.

Photo Finish

Date

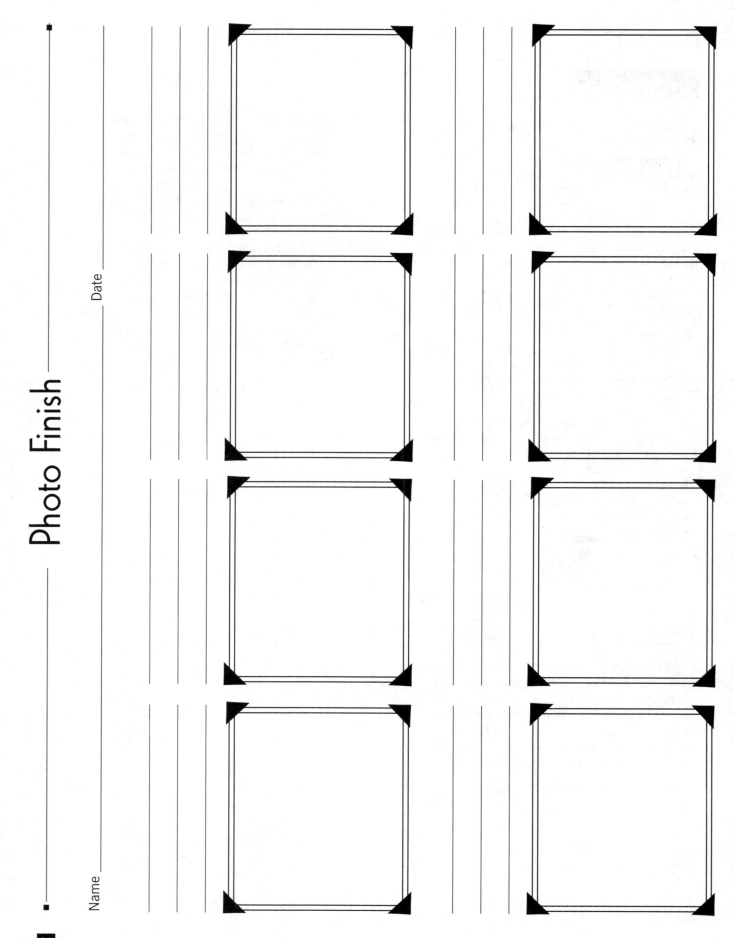

25 Quick Formative Assessments for a Differentiated Classroom • © 2009 by Judith Dodge • Scholastic Teaching Resources

Filming the Ideas

One of my students' favorite activities through-out the years has been using the Filming the Ideas organizer. Students like it because it gives them an opportunity to draw. I like it because it gives me an open window into my students' minds. They are required not only to draw, but to use very precise language in their writing.

This two-page organizer has eight boxes on each page, four on the left side and four on the right. The pages are stapled together, and students cut apart the boxes on top so they can be folded over to reveal the boxes underneath. This layered tool can be used to illustrate many organizational patterns of thought, such as cause and effect, compare and contrast, and sequence. Students can write a summary on one page and create a visual rendering on the other; the completed organizer can serve as an effective study tool.

It is important to include assessments with constructed responses in your repertoire, as anyone familiar with state assessments will tell you. Boxes on the first page of the Filming the Ideas organizer can be preprinted with constructed response questions that require students to apply their knowledge and skills to answer a question or complete a task. Students must write short answers or more extended responses on the second page. In this case, students would draw a simple sketch to illustrate the concept on the first page next to the constructed response question. On the second, lined page underneath, they would answer the question. Although assessments like these are more difficult to evaluate than assessments that simply require students to select a multiple-choice, true-false, matching, or short-answer fill-in from a provided list, formative assessments of this type contribute to more valid insights about student understanding (Ainsworth & Viegut, 2006).

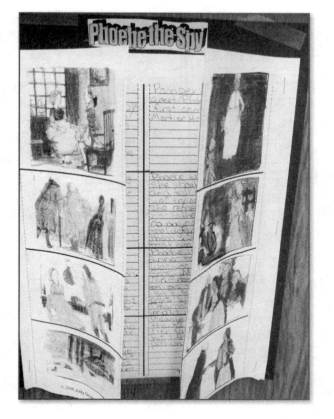

The Filming the Ideas organizer allows students in this classroom to keep track of the events occurring in the book their class is reading. (This template is available on the CD.)

1. Decide whether you are going to print the first page with questions and/or images or leave it blank.

2. Photocopy the Filming the Ideas reproducibles (pages 71–72) or have students bring up the digital copy on their computers.

3. Have students staple the eight-box unlined template on top of the eight-box lined template. Instruct them to place three or four staples along the outside margins. Then, students (or the teacher) can cut the top sheet along the middle bold line. This will allow the top sheet with questions and pictures to open up and reveal student-written responses. (To save time, you can instruct students to complete the cutting at home. The horizontal bold lines can be cut up to the side margins so that each box flips open separately.)

4. Give students clear directions about how to complete the assessment. Explain to students that the Filming the Ideas organizer will help them arrange ideas in ways that will make the information memorable. Be sure to explain which higher-level thinking skill the organizer will be used to illustrate. Will students be required to show cause and effect, compare and contrast, or problem-solution, by illustrating and labeling both the left and right sides of the organizer with these terms? Will students be asked to sequence events, describe change over time, record steps in a process, or note stages/phases/parts of a cycle by numbering the boxes from left to right continuing down the page?

5. Tell students if they have to include certain content vocabulary, show a particular number of steps, compare and contrast certain elements or factors, or sketch specific items or processes.

6. Allow students the time it takes for them to complete the required task. Depending on the way you design the activity, they may need a full class period (30–40 minutes) and/or additional time the next day or as homework. This type of assessment will take longer to finish than many of the others suggested in this book. However, keep in mind that by varying the type and complexity of the assessments you choose, you will have better and more accurate evidence of student understanding.

The Filming the Ideas organizer is frequently used to compare and contrast. Here, the student compares the Mesa Verde to his own community.

Use the Filming the Ideas organizer to teach the following skills and organizational patterns.

Chapter Summaries—Filming the Ideas is ideal for helping students create chapter summaries of classroom read-alouds (chapter books) or outside readings. If there are no titles for the chapters, ask students to create a title and a symbol or image that shows what each chapter is mostly about (main idea).

Describing a Concept—Students can use Filming the Ideas to represent their understanding of a concept by sharing facts, examples, characteristics, functions, or attributes of the concept, along with visuals. (For example, students can describe the digestive system by recording facts about it, providing examples of different types of digestion, describing its function and how it works, specifying characteristics of an unhealthy digestive system, etc.).

Recording Steps in a Process/Stages in a Cycle—Students can use Filming the Ideas to illustrate and show their understanding of stages in a life cycle, phases of the moon, steps in an experiment, or any other process or cycle.

Noting Events in Chronological Order/Sequence—Filming the Ideas is effective in social studies classrooms, where students can sequence historical events or record periods of history along with illustrations. It also can be used in language arts classrooms as a prewriting tool for creative writing (planning events in the story) or as an organizer for logical, coherent writing involving sequence (an autobiography, a character's change over time, events that impact a character's life, and so on).

Cause and Effect—Use the Filming the Ideas organizer when asking students to show understanding of cause-effect relationships. Label the four boxes on the left side of the top page with the word "Cause." Accompanying illustrations on this side of the page will show student understanding of each cause. Label the four boxes on the right side of the top page with the word "Effect." Illustrations on the right side will show student understanding of the effect of each cause to its left. Students will provide written explanations on the second page to describe each cause-effect relationship.

Compare and Contrast—The design of the Filming the Ideas organizer is also useful to compare and contrast any two ideas, concepts, periods of time, books, characters, groups, or classifications. On the left side, list four characteristics, elements, or factors. Students will illustrate the first page and elaborate in writing on the second page. On the right side, students will compare these characteristics, elements, or factors to those from a different time period, book, character, group, or classification.

Math Problem Solving—One of the best variations that evolved from teacher use of the Filming the Ideas organizer is the one-page, four-box version for solving word problems in math (see sample on page 70). Photocopy the organizer with the word problem printed in the first box. Then, model for the whole class how to solve the word problem by proceeding through the steps: recording known information and what needs to be solved; drawing an illustration of the data; solving and labeling the problem; and using the language of math to explain the procedure.

After you have modeled the steps for the entire class, allow students who have the confidence to proceed on their own to solve a second, similar problem which you have photocopied on the reverse side. Invite students who struggle with solving word problems to work with you around a table to solve the second problem together. Challenge advanced math students to create and solve their own word problem on a blank math Filming the Ideas organizer.

Use Transition Words With Filming the Ideas

▼

Be sure to introduce and require the use of transition words that are associated with each type of organizational pattern. Provide a list of transitions like the ones found in the Appendix (page 94) each time your students use Filming the Ideas. Post the words on your walls to reinforce their use during classroom conversations. (Allow them to place stickers with their initials on the posters whenever they use the words to communicate ideas.) Encourage students to use several transition words in any writing activity to help them connect their ideas. You can teach students to think more critically about information by helping them to arrange their thoughts using graphic organizers, along with appropriate transition words.

Problem

Cathy loves to bake cookies. She bakes 67 chocolate chip cookies. She wants to put them into bags with 8 cookies in each bag. How many bags will she need? Will she have any cookies leftover? If so, how many? If she puts the leftover cookies in another bag, then how many bags will she need?

What I know — What I Need to Find Out

- 67 cookies
- 8 cookies per bag

How many bags?
Any leftover cookies? How many?
How many bags if you add one for the leftovers

Illustration

Solve & Label

bags 8 R3 - leftovers
cookies per bag 8)67 cookies
64
03

8 bags
+
a bag for leftovers

9 bags

Explain and Justify

First I divided the 67 cookies by 8 because 8 cookies go in each bag. I got 8 which means there are 8 bags. There were 3 leftovers so I added another bag to put the leftovers in. There is a total of 9 bags.

The Filming the Ideas for Math problem-solving invites students who have difficulty with word problems approach them with less anxiety. This student-friendly graphic helps a learner break down the problem into manageable steps and encourages illustrations. (This template is available on the CD.)

Tips for Tiering!

In addition to the ideas on page 9, consider the following.

To support struggling learners: Supply a simpler list of transition words for students to choose from (i.e., *first, second, next, then, later, soon, after that, finally*).

Preprint the Filming the Ideas organizer with the transition words in each box.

To challenge advanced learners: After giving general directions, leave the task more open-ended.

Allow students to create their own questions to answer.

Provide an advanced list of transition words (*initially, subsequently, simultaneously, consequently,* and so on) for them to choose from.

Require students to compare and contrast the new information with something they studied before (without suggesting the comparisons).

Have students research new information related to the topic and organize it in one of the patterns described on page 69 under Applications.

TechConnect

Use Kid Pix, VoiceThread, Photo Story, Movie Maker, or PowerPoint to integrate technology with this assessment tool. (See TechConnect Ideas from previous chapters for brief descriptions and URLs to learn about some of these technologies.)

Name _____ | Date _____

"Filming the Ideas" © Judith Dodge

"Filming the Ideas" © Judith Dodge

25 Quick Formative Assessments for a Differentiated Classroom • © 2009 by Judith Dodge • Scholastic Teaching Resources

Flipbooks

It's been my experience that most students love to draw. Giving these students the opportunity to draw in a content-area classroom usually evokes great enthusiasm and involvement in the task. Since drawing pictures or symbolic representations of information stimulates and increases activity in the brain (Gerlic & Jausovec, 1999), there is good reason for us to provide students with opportunities to create such nonlinguistic representations.

A Flipbook, which includes both linguistic and nonlinguistic elements, is an ideal tool for encouraging elaboration of information. Students are asked to draw as well as write about the information being studied in a layered book (Zike, 2004). While verbal/linguistic learners will prefer to write about the information, spatial learners will prefer to illustrate their understanding. The flipbook requires both forms of expression. Therefore, you will be able to assess the learning of your students more accurately, whatever their preference.

Step-by-Step

1. Have students take three pieces of 8½" x 11" paper and layer them vertically, stepping each page down ¾" at a time.

2. Have students align the papers neatly on both sides. Instruct students to hold the three pages on both sides by placing their thumbs underneath the three pages and their other fingers on top. Have them fold all three sheets upward in one motion, stepping down ¾" inch one more time. All the tabs are the same distance apart. Students will now have a flipbook with five ¾" tabs and a larger top fold to be used as a cover.

3. When the first five tabs are the same distance apart, have students crease the papers well.

4. Have students turn the booklet so the crease is at the top. Place two staples on the top of the booklet.

5. To design a Mini-Flipbook, have students follow steps 1-3, then cut the booklet in half. For a neater cut, you may want students to first use a ruler and mark 4¼" on two or three spots. Have them lightly sketch a line down the middle of the booklet and then cut it in half. Alternatively, you can use a paper cutter ahead of time to cut all of the paper in half. Have them staple each booklet at the crease.

6. The Flipbook is now ready for use.

7. On the ¾" tabs have students write subtopics, concepts, or questions that you provide. Then, tell them to lift the flap above and write what they know about the subtopic/concept or answer the question. On the flipped page above, they will illustrate their understanding.

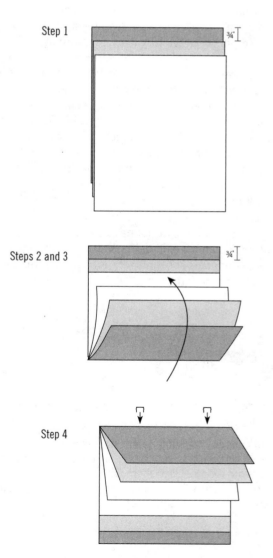

Step 1

Steps 2 and 3

Step 4

When we choose to use a Flipbook for assessment, we do so because we want to create a unique opportunity to enhance student elaboration. Keep in mind, however, that some students will simply be unable to illustrate as a way of showing understanding. Therefore, as with Photo Finish, and other nonlinguistic assessments, we must be careful not to interpret their lack of artistic skills as lack of understanding about the concepts. Be sure to explain to students that you will look at their whole Flipbook—words and pictures—to assess their understanding and to measure what they have come to know.

Applications

Aside from providing valuable assessment data, the Flipbook will serve as a great study tool for students later on. As they both draw illustrations and elaborate in words, students are reorganizing information that they have learned. This reorganization is the essence of a good study strategy. When we reorganize previously learned information, we are more likely to place it in long-term memory.

Students love to make the Mini-Flipbooks (see step 5 on page 73 for directions on making them). In many classrooms, they often choose to make one on "Choice Homework Night" (Dodge, 2005), when they have the option of choosing from several activities to show what they know in a way they prefer. If you punch a hole on the top of the small booklet, it can be kept neatly in a student's binder.

While most teachers are familiar with basic flipbooks (which offer descriptions of topics or concepts), you might not have thought of using the Flipbook as a visual time line (showing change over time, sequence of events, etc.), as a Venn diagram (showing comparison and contrast), or to show pros and cons or cause and effect. By turning the Flipbook (or the Mini-Flipbook) on its side, it becomes a visual time line, providing students a clear sense of sequence or chronology.

To design a Flipbook that shows comparison and contrast, pros and cons, or cause and effect, follow steps 1–4. Then, cut the pages in half, leaving the back page uncut. The back page will hold the booklet together. Now you can compare the differences between two books, time periods, countries, biomes, systems, and so on, according to different characteristics (see sample on page 75). On the back of the Flipbook, students can record how the two things being compared are the same.

Similarly, by labeling one side "Advantages" and the other side "Disadvantages," students can use this cut flipbook to show their understanding of the pros and cons of a particular document, treaty, governmental policy, presidency, solution to a problem, and so forth.

Finally, you can also use this two-part Flipbook to describe the cause and effect of actions and events.

Tips for Tiering!

In addition to the ideas on page 9, consider the following.

To support struggling learners: Provide students with out-of-sequence sentence strips that have descriptions, steps, or events. Have them sequence the ideas, copy or paste them into their Flipbook, and then draw an illustration to represent each one.

To challenge advanced learners: Instead of providing students with subtopics, steps, and questions to use in their Flipbooks, tell them only what the assessment is designed to show (for example: *cause and effect of different weather conditions, comparing and contrasting different geographical regions, the change over time of the main character*), and let them organize the Flipbook in any way they choose in order to show this information.

Flipbooks Can Assess Student Understanding in the Following Areas:

LANGUAGE ARTS:
- Writing more complex sentences
- Beginning, middle, end
- Change over time
- Sequence/steps
- Compare and contrast
- Cause-effect (motivation-effect)
- Descriptions and examples of characters/themes/story elements/literary devices/conflicts, etc.

SCIENCE:
- Observations over time
- Sequence/steps in an experiment
- Stages in a life cycle
- Compare and contrast
- Cause and effect
- Advantages and disadvantages
- Descriptions and examples of ecosystems, organisms, human systems, weather systems, forces/energy/resources, etc.

SOCIAL STUDIES:
- Change over time
- Sequence of events/steps leading to…
- Compare and contrast
- Cause and effect
- Advantages and disadvantages
- Descriptions and examples of key historical figures/major contributions/turning points/important events/civilizations/documents/issues/political groups/time periods, etc.

TechConnect

TechConnect: At one of the best Web sites for teacher resources on reading, the International Reading Association's ReadWriteThink.org, you can design a flipbook online and print it out, ready to go.

For more info:
http://www.readwritethink.org/materials/flipbook/.

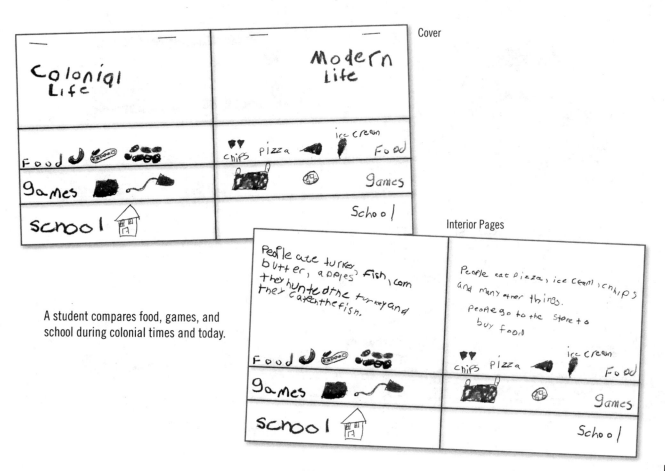

A student compares food, games, and school during colonial times and today.

SmartCards

SmartCards are a collection of student-written summaries and illustrations on index cards about subtopics or concepts from one unit of study. Although at first glance they may look like flash cards, these summary cards require higher levels of thinking than flash cards generally do. While flash cards usually include just a word, a definition, and, perhaps, an example or picture, SmartCards require students to get the "big picture" of an idea and condense it into their own words (Agee, 2008). In addition, they require students to summarize ideas from class, textbooks, or homework assignments, rephrasing things because this helps students to master the concepts (Conner, 2006).

SmartCards, however, are more than just summaries; they serve as excellent assessment tools for learning. Students complete them one at a time throughout an entire unit of study, and you can collect them at any time to assess student understanding. After reading the cards over and writing brief comments on them, you return them to students so that the cards might be layered as a set of SmartCards about one main topic (see example below and illustration on page 77). By reading the cards, you should have a good idea of what students know up to this point.

The SmartCards created for this unit on simple machines serve as a study tool for review.

1. Hand out one piece of heavy-stock paper to each student. (You can also use manila folders.) Have students label the top of the heavy-stock paper with the main topic under study, or the title of a book being read (for example: "Biomes," "*The BFG*"). Students will attach index cards to this sheet to make up a set of SmartCards on a specific main topic or book.

2. Now have students write the name of the first subtopic or question that you provide on the bottom of the unlined side of the card (for example: "The Rain Forest," "Characters"). Each card will represent a different subtopic of the main topic. (The second subtopic might be: "The Desert" or "Setting.")

3. Decide as a class what the front of the card (unlined side) should include to represent the information. *Will there be a web with subtopics on the spokes? Should there be drawings to make the concept memorable? What illustrations could we include? Might we list essential questions to consider?*

4. After brainstorming as a whole class what graphic organizer, illustrations, or essential questions should be placed on the front of the card, you can let students work together in pairs to discuss what written details (terms, definitions, examples, etc.) need to be included on the lined back of the card. If time is short, you can then assign the second side of the SmartCard for homework.

5. You can collect this completed SmartCard the following day and make notes about any misunderstandings or gaps in student understanding. Write brief comments as feedback to your students.

6. Let students pair-share to discuss their cards and borrow ideas from one another to make their SmartCards more complete.

7. Finally, have students tape their card (with the unlined side and labeled subtopic face up) at the bottom of the heavy paper mentioned in Step 1. Future cards will be layered on top of this card. (See below.)

Front view

Main Topic_____
Subtopic 3
Subtopic 2
Subtopic 1

Inside view

Subtopic 3
Subtopic 2
Subtopic 1

Applications

Some teachers keep these cards in a file drawer for their students and return them before quarterly, mid-term, or final exams. This is especially helpful to students who are disorganized or those who tend to lose many of their important papers. The SmartCards make studying for these exams much easier than starting from scratch with traditional review sessions.

Occasionally, teachers will allow students to use their cards on a summative assessment that follows. This is a good way to impress upon stu-dents the value of creating accurate and complete SmartCards throughout the unit. Students usually put extra effort into the set of cards they prepare for a subsequent unit, hoping they can once again use them during the summative assessment. This time, you can either allow them to use their cards during the test, allow them to study from the cards for a few minutes before the test, or give them from one to five bonus points on the test, depending upon how complete and accurate the SmartCards are.

Tips for Tiering!

In addition to the ideas on page 9, consider the following.

To support struggling learners: Give students a list of questions, terms, and sketches (on a checklist) to be included on their SmartCard.

To challenge advanced learners: Provide a blank card. Encourage these students to syn-thesize the information any way they think best.

TechConnect

At StudyStack, you can have students create digital sets of flash cards with which they can practice online or export to their iPods for on-the-go practice!

For more info: www.studystack.com.

This fourth grader is eager to work on her SmartCards on the plant life cycle.

Section 4

Collaborative Activities

The formative assessment strategies that follow ask students to collaborate with others and orally describe what they are learning. Most of the strategies also involve movement, making these assessment strategies special favorites of most students. Carla Hannaford, in her book *Smart Moves: Why Learning Is Not All in Your Head* (1995), explains that movement is essential to learning. *"Movement awakens and activates many of our mental capacities.* Movement integrates and anchors new information and experience into our neural networks. And movement is vital to all the actions by which we embody and express our learning, our understanding and ourselves." Focusing on bodily-kinesthetic and interpersonal skills, the five assessment strategies that follow invite greater engagement and communication as students journey toward mastery of content.

Turn 'n' Talk

This strategy encourages student conversation about what they are learning. Based loosely on Dr. Mary Budd Rowe's *10-2 Structure* (1986), it calls for students to listen for ten minutes to the teacher's presentation and then to discuss for two minutes with a partner their notes and understandings about the topic. This can be repeated several times during a lesson. During the last few minutes of the class, the teacher brings all students back together; students summarize key understandings, and the teacher sorts out misconceptions.

Eric Jensen (1996) describes how researchers have come to see that attentiveness runs in cycles and that it lessens after just a brief time of focus (from 5 to 20 minutes in most school-age children). To influence students' attention, you can limit your lectures and activities, and follow with a two-to-five-minute "diffusion" activity (a total break from the content or an alternative form of the learning) that refocuses attention. Diffusion activities may include partner shares, student presentations, creation of individual graphic organizers, group work, or even relaxation exercises and Simon Says stretch breaks.

Step-by-Step

1. After approximately 10–15 minutes of class discussion or lecture, have students turn to a partner. Younger students should discuss what is most important to remember, perhaps listing key ideas together on paper. Older students should share their own notes and discuss the main ideas of this segment of class instruction.

2. During this time, circulate among the pairs, asking questions to check more deeply for understanding.

3. Bring the whole class back together. Point out any confusion or gaps in knowledge that you have become aware of.

4. Continue with the lesson for another 10–15 minutes. Repeat the opportunity for Turn n' Talk.

Applications

Use Turn 'n' Talk as a diffusion activity, as well as a strategy for longer retention. Use it when you see glazed eyes, confusion, or signs of boredom in your students. This quick strategy will reenergize and refocus them.

TechConnect

To use the Turn 'n' Talk strategy as a digital formative assessment, pose a series of questions to which students must respond on their laptops (or on a computer in a computer lab). After each question, allow partners one minute to discuss their answers first. Then, have each student individually respond to the question online using SurveyMonkey. You and your class will be able to view the results graphically in real time and you will be able to analyze the data for subsequent instruction.

For more info: www.surveymonkey.com.

Tips for Tiering!

In addition to the ideas on page 9, consider the following.

To support struggling learners: Provide students with an outline to guide their discussion. For example, you can partially fill in Noting What I've Learned, found on page 46.

Provide a list of questions (on a handout) that partners should ask each other to help keep the Turn 'n' Talk conversation focused and moving along. (See page 81; cut into quarters and give one to each set of partners.)

To challenge advanced learners: Ask students to generate questions and answers that can be used with the entire class for review.

Turn 'n' Talk

- What are the most important ideas to remember?

- What are some of the details related to each idea?

- What questions do we need to ask so that we can understand this information better?

- How is this information related to something else we know?

- What are the most important ideas to remember?

- What are some of the details related to each idea?

- What questions do we need to ask so that we can understand this information better?

- How is this information related to something else we know?

- What are the most important ideas to remember?

- What are some of the details related to each idea?

- What questions do we need to ask so that we can understand this information better?

- How is this information related to something else we know?

- What are the most important ideas to remember?

- What are some of the details related to each idea?

- What questions do we need to ask so that we can understand this information better?

- How is this information related to something else we know?

Headline News! Summary

CONVICTION OVERTURNED! (New Information Emerges)	**SOUNDS OF A BUBBLE BURSTING** (Foreclosures in the Wake of the Real Estate Bust)
FAILURE TO ACT!! (Investigative Report on the Railroad System)	**HOPES DASHED FOR TRUCE!** (Two Sides Fail to Come to Agreement Despite International Urging)
THE WAIT IS OVER!! (Release of a New Anti-Cancer Drug by the FDA)	

The Headline News! Summary asks students to sum up the essence of a lesson by creating newspaper headlines and delivering a brief news summary as an innovative way to involve them in meaning making. Allowed to use only a few words in the headline, students must think of a concise way to summarize what they have learned. Small-group discussions provide them with the opportunity to reflect upon what they have heard, read, or seen immediately following the learning experience. Allowing students to have small-group discussions helps learners make connections they may not make on their own.

Step-by-Step

1. Familiarize students with headlines and their purpose. In *Differentiation in Action* (Dodge, 2005), I describe a process to help students get comfortable with creating headlines. The process familiarizes the whole class with headlines they see in the newspaper.

2. Place students in small groups to create their own headlines for articles that you provide (with the headlines cut off).

3. Model for the entire class how to apply this summarizing technique to developing "headlines" for a passage from a novel or social studies or science textbook.

4. Ask pairs to create headlines for subsequent passages in the textbook.

5. Have partners share their ideas with the whole class, alternating between the reading/writing activity for a passage and the sharing.

6. You will need to model for students how to write a summary. You can use the following questions to guide your whole-class practice with summarizing: *What is the main idea? What do we know so far? What is the significance of the event, discovery, problem, conflict, etc.? Whom does it affect? What seems likely for the future?*

7. You can provide additional practice for homework. Over time, students' ability to summarize the essence of a reading or class discussion will become more refined.

8. Once students are comfortable with writing headlines, you can give small groups a few minutes during class to prepare an oral summary of the event, chapter, passage, or concept in a one- or two-minute Headline News! Summary. You might want to provide sentence starters such as the following to guide the development of their summary:

> "What we know so far is…" "At this point, we understand that…"
>
> "The conflict appears to be…" "The action taken by… has led to…"
>
> "The problems facing us now are…" "What remains to be seen is…"

(Adapted from Jeffrey Wilhelm's *Action Strategies for Deepening Comprehension*, Scholastic, 2002)

You can have students in small groups develop the Headline News! Summary first. Then they can work to develop the headline. For some students (those who are right-brained, preferring steps that go from whole to part), this process might be easier.

Create a Headline News! bulletin board in your classroom so that your students can post their headlines summarizing what they've learned. This bulletin board should remain in place for the entire year, if possible, to help students see all of the learning that has taken place. In addition, the bulletin board will help students activate prior knowledge when they try to make connections to new material they are studying.

Tips for Tiering!

In addition to the ideas on page 9, consider the following.

To support struggling learners: Provide an outline for a written script for Headline News! Summary.

Offer a selection of topics from which to choose. Then, have students write the Headline News! Summary from an outline or sentence starters.

To challenge advanced learners: Place an advanced group of readers/writers together and ask them to:

- use puns, metaphors, or similes as part of their headlines

- predict a future event in their headline, based on what they know so far, then write the Headline News! Summary as if the prediction has taken place

- create two headlines showing opposing viewpoints on the same subject

TechConnect

Using the Web site listed below, your students can work alone or with one or two others to create a one-page newspaper article with as many as to three headlines and articles. They can customize the name, fonts, colors, and layout for their digital Headline News! Summary.

Go to: http://interactives.mped.org/view_interactive.aspx?id=110&title

Headline News! Summary

Name _____ Date _____

News Subject _____

The Headline:

```
┌─────────────────────────────────────────────────────────┐
│                                                         │
│                                                         │
│                                                         │
│                                                         │
│                                                         │
│                                                         │
└─────────────────────────────────────────────────────────┘
```

Consider the following: _____

- What is the main idea?
- What do we know so far?
- What is the significance of the event, discovery, problem, conflict, etc.?

- Whom does it affect?
- What seems likely for the future?

The Summary:

```
┌─────────────────────────────────────────────────────────┐
│ _____  │
│ _____  │
│ _____  │
│ _____  │
│ _____  │
│ _____  │
│ _____  │
│ _____  │
│ _____  │
└─────────────────────────────────────────────────────────┘
```

Group Members:

- _____   - _____

- _____   - _____

Four More!

Four More! is an assessment tool for closure that integrates collaboration, movement, and individual accountability. Students who struggle to stay seated all day long will welcome this movement activity.

The strategy begins with students working on their own. They then move around the classroom for a brief period of interaction and information gathering with classmates. The movement part of the activity usually takes no longer than three or four minutes, but it is just enough time to reenergize students and allow them to refocus their attention at the end of a lesson. Then, students head back to their seats where they individually elaborate upon what they've recorded, adding details to the main ideas they have gathered from their peers.

This animated learner enjoys the interaction that is encouraged as part of the Four More! activity. (This template is available on the CD.)

The second part of the Four More! activity invites individual reflection on what they have learned while engaging with their peers.

1. Tell students that it's time to summarize what they have been learning today. Give each student a Four More! template (page 87).

2. Have all students write two key ideas (main ideas) that they recall from the lesson on the lines in the first two boxes.

3. Now, have students move from their desks to circulate with peers. Tell them they must gather four more ideas, one additional idea from each of four *different* students to fill the remaining boxes.

Explain that completing this idea-sharing part of the task is very important for their next activity and that they will have approximately three minutes to collect ideas from classmates. Encourage students to move around the room, and advise them to return to their seats as soon as they are done.

4. When all students are seated again (or when you call "time" after about three minutes), ask students to elaborate individually on the main ideas by providing at least two details or descriptions next to the bullets for each key idea.

Applications

Use this strategy to review for a unit test or as a prewriting activity for an upcoming essay.

Four More!

Concept/Topic: The Atlantic Provinces of Canada

Key Idea: (On your own, jot a key idea)
Acadians were exiled.

- Britian feared that French Acadians might secretly be loyal to France.
- Some exiled Acadians settled in Quebec or New Brunswick.

Key Idea: (On your own, jot a key idea)
Fishing is a major industry.

- The fishing industry has changed.
- The government banned cod fishing.

Key Idea:
1. Fishing made industries grow in the 1800s.

- Region led Canada in ship construction through most of the 1800s.
- Forestry and fishing industries helped the region's economy boom.

Key Idea:
2. The Atlantic Provinces are also called the Maritime Provinces.

- It is by the sea.
- Economy is based on fish.

Key Idea:
3. The Atlantic Provinces are along the coast.

- Much of the economy depends on fishing.
- Also called the Maritime Provinces.

Key Idea:
4. Prince Edward Island, New Brunswick, and Nova Scotia make up the Atlantic Provinces.

- Located in eastern Canada.
- The population of the Atlantic Provinces is 1,835,730.

This Four More! summarizer was used after students were assigned a textbook reading on the Atlantic Provinces of Canada. After jotting down two key ideas of their own, students collaborated with peers to find Four More!, and returned to their seats to elaborate further on their own.

Four More!

Name _____ Date _____

Key Idea: (On your own, jot a key idea)

_____

_____

_____

_____

❑

❑

Key Idea: (On your own, jot a key idea)

_____

_____

_____

_____

❑

❑

Key Idea:

1. _____

_____

_____

_____

❑

❑

Key Idea:

2. _____

_____

_____

_____

❑

❑

Key Idea:

3. _____

_____

_____

_____

❑

❑

Key Idea:

4. _____

_____

_____

_____

❑

❑

Find Someone Who… Review

Find Someone Who … Review is another movement activity that focuses on content while inviting student interaction that is purposeful. Students reinforce their learning by explaining what they know to others, who listen actively and agree or disagree. Moving throughout the classroom for about ten minutes, students will ask and answer nine questions and record the responses on their own charts.

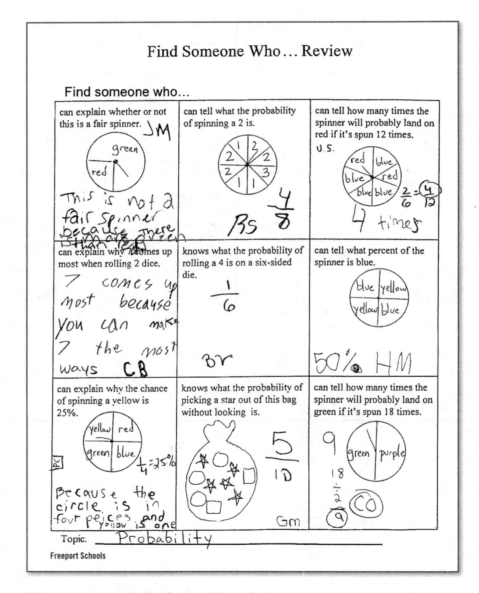

Find Someone Who… Review

Find someone who…

can explain whether or not this is a fair spinner. JM	can tell what the probability of spinning a 2 is.	can tell how many times the spinner will probably land on red if it's spun 12 times.
green, red — This is not a fair spinner because there...	$\frac{4}{8}$ RS	U.S. $\frac{2}{6} = \frac{4}{12}$ 4 times
can explain why 7 comes up most when rolling 2 dice.	knows what the probability of rolling a 4 is on a six-sided die.	can tell what percent of the spinner is blue.
7 comes up most because you can make 7 the most ways CB	$\frac{1}{6}$ or	50% HM
can explain why the chance of spinning a yellow is 25%.	knows what the probability of picking a star out of this bag without looking is.	can tell how many times the spinner will probably land on green if it's spun 18 times.
$\frac{1}{4} = 25\%$ Because the circle is in four peices and yellow is one	$\frac{5}{10}$ Gm	9 18 $\frac{2}{4}$ CO

Topic: Probability

Freeport Schools

Math students used this Find Someone Who … Review to process their understanding on the topic of probability. As students circulated and shared answers, they signed their initials in the box showing their response. (This template is available on the CD. In addition to a generic template for content-area classrooms, there is a template for use in developing student social skills, a getting-to-know-you activity.)

25 Quick Formative Assessments for a Differentiated Classroom • © 2009 by Judith Dodge • Scholastic Teaching Resources

Step-by-Step

1. Hand out copies of the Find Someone Who ... Review template (page 90). To save time, run the chart off with nine focus questions related to the present topic of study printed in each box.

2. Give students ten minutes to circulate through the room and ask their classmates for the answers to the questions on the sheet. Explain to them that each answer must come from a different student and remind them that as they're conducting their inquiries, they need to talk in quiet voices and to give the speaker their complete attention. Tell them to return to their desk when their charts are complete.

3. Circulate among students, taking note of student responses and assessing understanding.

4. After students return to their desks, ask them to synthesize what they have learned (or reviewed) by having them write a brief summary. The summaries provide an opportunity for students to reorganize the information, thus increasing the likelihood of retention.

Applications

This activity can be used to activate prior knowledge before beginning the study of a unit or a novel, or it can be used as a rehearsal strategy to process new information. Of course, it can also be used at the end of a unit to assess what students have learned.

In addition, this activity can be used as a review for a homework reading assignment. After circulating and talking about the reading, students are "primed" to analyze the reading more closely with the teacher.

This activity puts the responsibility on the students when used for test review. Students integrate what they've learned using interpersonal skills as well as relying on their own cognitive skills for creating summaries.

The Find Someone Who ... Review format can also be used to build social skills in your classroom. Instead of prompting students to review content, direct students to find out information about each other. A Find Someone Who ... Social Skills reproducible is available on the companion CD. As students mingle to find others who have similar interests, hobbies, collections, and dreams, they get to know their peers in a new way. It's enjoyable to use this activity at the beginning of the year, after a vacation, or near a holiday.

Find Someone Who ... Review

Name _____ Date _____

Topic _____

Find someone who:

can tell you when ...	can describe what would happen if ...	can explain why ...
can describe the difference between ...	can make a connection between ... and ...	can describe the effect of ...
can describe how ...	can explain the point of view of ...	can explain the sequence of ...

Carousel Brainstorming

Carousel Brainstorming is a powerful summarizing activity that engages all learners. As students "carousel" from chart to chart, they record ideas, details, and illustrations that show their understanding of a particular topic or concept. In heterogeneous groups, students brainstorm together for a few minutes about a topic or question before they "carousel" to the next chart. This assessment technique utilizes small groups and focused conversations that help build student confidence. Used as an assessment, Carousel Brainstorming allows you to get a feel for what the class has learned and pinpoint any gaps or misunderstandings.

These eager learners worked together as a team, rotating from chart to chart as they analyzed their reading in a Carousel Brainstorm activity.

Step-by-Step

1. Create a list of important subtopics or open-ended questions about your big topic. Write each one on a different sheet of chart paper. You can use the planning sheet on page 93.

2. Form groups of students so that there are as many groups as there are charts. For example, if you created five charts, you should have five groups. (Form groups by having students count off from 1 to 5 and then grouping all the 1s together, all the 2s together, and so on.)

3. Number the charts to indicate the order in which groups should move from chart to chart. Make sure, however, that the charts themselves do not build upon one another, because some students will be starting at the last charts and then moving to the first charts.

4. Give a different color marker to each group and have the groups "carousel" from chart to chart and respond in writing to each of the topics or questions. For each chart, a different group member records the group's responses on the chart. Students might draw a sketch or a symbol to illustrate an idea, provide details or examples for each subtopic,

perform a required mathematics operation, or answer a provided question with a response that is different from those already recorded.

5. Explain to your students that they must read what others have written but may not directly copy what's already been said (although, to encourage language development, you might allow them to say the same thing in a different way or to elaborate on another group's response by adding additional words).

6. Give students from two to three minutes at each chart to add as many ideas as they can, and then ring a bell or flick the light to signal that it's time to move to the next chart.

7. The Carousel Brainstorming strategy is an activity for processing and reviewing information. Be sure to provide a follow-up activity that makes use of the information gathered. Using the charts, students can write brief essays that note relationships, summarize information, or make comparisons. The charts can be referred to by the whole class. The teacher should point out errors or misunderstandings and provide additional information where he/she has noticed gaps in understandings.

Topics for Carousel Brainstorming

- Shapes
- Colors
- Money
- Time
- Making numbers
- Animals
- Letters

- Word study
- Analyzing graphs
- Different ways to make the number ____
- Story elements
- Comparing fairy tales
- Expanding sentences
- Character analysis

- Study of the decades
- Comparison of body systems
- Elements of a civilization
- Presidents
- The Civil War (causes and effects, battles, the Underground Railroad, historical figures)

A Sample Lesson:

Using Carousel Brainstorming to Provide Student Practice in Analyzing Graphs

Teach a mini-lesson to the whole class on how to analyze graphs.

Form heterogeneous groups for a Carousel Brainstorming. Each chart should have a different graph (photocopied and attached to the chart) for students to analyze with their group. They will rotate through the charts, drawing conclusions about each graph (or answering open-ended questions that you have written on the charts).

After students return to their desks, give each an Exit Card with a new graph on it and ask students to analyze the graph on their own. Collect, assess, and determine what instruction and grouping need to take place the next day.

Applications

You can use the charts as a prewriting activity. Students can be asked to write a summary using information from all of the charts or to compare and contrast information on two of the charts (two presidents, two characters, two stories, two time periods, and so on).

If the charts are about characterization, you might ask students to stand next to the character they are most like (or most unlike) and explain how they are similar or different using details from the charts.

TechConnect

To integrate technology, use computer stations or laptops instead of charts around the room. (If you have a Smart Board, students can save their charts in Word and send them to the Smart Board. The charts can then be saved in Smart Board Notebook software for printing copies and future retrieval.) At each computer, open and save a Word document with a different question or subtopic for the Carousel Brainstorming. As small groups of students rotate through all the computer stations, they must print their response using their own color at each station. You can print out the responses from all the stations and provide students with their own copies to use for follow-up writing assignments.

Tips for Tiering!

In addition to the ideas on page 9, consider the following.

To support struggling learners: Provide them with details written on sticky notes. Have them place the notes on the appropriate charts.

Encourage students to draw illustrations on the charts.

Buddy-up shy or quiet students (or ELLs) with a partner.

To challenge advanced learners: Ask students to create symbols to represent main concepts and themes.

Concept/Topic _____

Key understandings (what students must know and/or be able to do):

■

■

■

Create four to six open-ended questions or subtopics that will prompt students to share what they know about the key understandings they should be developing about the topic. Record these here, then write each on a separate sheet of chart paper for students to work with as described on page 92.

Chart 1:	Chart 2:
Chart 3:	Chart 4:
Chart 5:	Chart 6:

Tips for Making the Carousel Brainstorming Strategy Work

■ Design questions/subtopics that are open-ended, allowing for an unlimited number of responses.

■ Include no more than five members in a group.

■ Provide a different-color marker for each group.

■ After two to three minutes, rotate the groups.

■ Have the marker rotate with the group.

■ Rotate the recorder at each chart.

■ Remind students that they
  • must read what previous groups have written.
  • may not repeat what has been written.

• may add an asterisk or exclamation point if they agree strongly with a prior group's response.

• may write a question mark next to or circle a prior group's response. (This will increase the likelihood of accuracy on the charts and pinpoint areas of confusion to be reviewed.)

■ Use the charts for a written follow-up activity with students. (For example: *Choose the character with whom you most identify. Compare and contrast yourself with this character in at least three ways.*)

Appendix

■ ■ ■ ■ ■ ■ ■ ■ ■ ■ ■ ■ ■ ■ ■ ■

Transition Words

The transition words below can be used with Web Wind-Up, Matrix, Filming the Ideas, and any other graphic organizer to evoke logical and coherent writing as a follow-up about a topic.

USE TRANSITION WORDS TO ...

Describe a Concept (the language of "addition")

First	Second	The third reason
And	For one thing	To further illustrate
Also	In addition	A third way
Another	Another way	Furthermore
For instance	Another example	Another similarity
For example	Besides	Finally

Compare and Contrast

Both	Also	Neither
Each	Same	Much as
Similarly	Different	And
In common	Whereas	On the contrary
One difference	In comparison	But
Even though	However	Although
Similar to	Instead	
In the same way	In contrast	

Show Chronology/Sequence/Steps/Stages

At first	Then	Finally
Long ago	Soon	Eventually
Looking back	Later	Lastly
To begin with	Before long	Subsequently
In the beginning	After that	Consequently
First	Last	In the future
Earlier	At the same time	Years from now
First ... Second ... Third ... etc.	Meanwhile	
Next	While	

Illustrate Cause and Effect:

As a result	Since	Thus
Because	Due to	If ... then
For this reason	Since	Then ... so
So	This led to	
Therefore	Consequently	

Reproducibles Index

All forms are available on the companion CD

Section 1: Summaries and Reflections

Section 2: Lists, Charts, and Graphic Organizers

Section 3: Visual Representations of Information

Section 4: Collaborative Activities

Tip

To view and print the files on the CD, you will need to download Adobe Reader™, version 7.0 or higher. This download is available free of charge for Mac and PC systems at www.adobe.com/products/acrobat/readstep2.

Bibliography

Agee, K. *Concept cards.* University of California at Merced. Retrieved spring 2008 from http://learning.ucmerced.edu/docs/conceptcards.doc

Ainsworth, L., & Viegut, D. (2006). *Common formative assessments: How to connect standards-based instruction and assessment.* Thousand Oaks, CA: Corwin.

Atwell, N. (1990). *Coming to know: Writing to learn in the intermediate grades.* Portsmouth, NH: Heineman.

Berk, L., & Winsler, A. (1995). *Scaffolding children's learning: Vygotsky and early childhood education.* Washington, D.C.: National Association for the Education of Young Children.

Chappuis, S., & Chappuis, J. (2007/2008, December/January). The best value in formative assessment. *Educational Leadership, 65,* 14-18.

Conner, J. (2006). *Concept cards.* Indiana University. Retrieved spring 2008 from http://www.indiana.edu/~l517/concept_cards.htm

D/Angelo; F. (2007). Dividing by two and five. *Articles for Educators.* Retrieved summer 2007 from http://articlesforeducators.com/dir/mathematics/division/two_and_five.asp

Dodge, J. (2005). *Differentiation in action.* New York: Scholastic.

Dodge, J. (1994). *The study skills handbook.* New York: Scholastic.

Fisher, D., & Frey, N. (2007). *Checking for understanding: Formative assessment techniques for your classroom.* Alexandria, VA: ASCD.

Gerlic, I., & Jausovec, N. (1999). Multimedia: Differences in cognitive processes observed with EEG. *Educational Technology Research and Development, 47,* 5-14.

Guskey, T. (2007/2008: December/January). The rest of the story. *Educational Leadership, 65,* 28-35.

Guskey, T. (2007). Using assessments to improve teaching and learning. In D. Reeves (Ed.), *Ahead of the curve: The power of assessment to transform teaching and learning.* Bloomington, Indiana: Solution Tree.

Hannaford, C. (1995). *Smart moves: Why learning is not all in your head.* Arlington, VA: Great Ocean, Inc.

Hyerle, D. (2000). *A field guide to using visual tools.* Alexandria, VA: ASCD.

Irwin-DeVitis, L., & Pease, D. (1995). Using graphic organizers for learning and assessment in middle level classrooms. *Middle School Journal, 26,* 57-64.

Irwin-DeVitis, L., Modlo, M., & Bromley, K. (1999). *50 graphic organizers for reading writing and more.* New York: Scholastic.

Jensen, E. (1996). *Brain-based learning.* Del Mar, California: Turning Point Publishing.

Marzano, R., Pickering, D., & Pollock, J. (2001). *Classroom instruction that works.* Alexandria, VA: ASCD.

Marzano, R. (2006). *Classroom assessment & grading that work.* Alexandria, VA: ASCD.

McKenzie, J. (1997, October). *From now on.* Retrieved summer 2007 from http://www.fno.org//oct97/grids.html#anchor652474

McLaughlin, M., & Vogt, M. (2000). *Creativity and innovation in content area teaching.* Norwood, MA: Christopher-Gordon.

Paivio, A. (1986). *Mental representations: a dual coding approach.* Oxford, England: Oxford University Press.

Parks, S., & Black, H. (1990). *Organizing thinking: Book I.* Pacific Grove, CA: Critical Thinking Press and Software.

Parks, S., & Black, H. (1990). *Organizing thinking: Book II.* Pacific Grove, CA: Critical Thinking Press and Software.

Pauk, W. (2000). *How to study in college.* Boston, MA: Houghton Mifflin.

Raphael, T. (1986). Teaching question-answer relationships, revisited. *The Reading Teacher, 39,* 516-522.

Rasinski, T., & Padak, N. (2000). *Effective reading strategies* (2nd ed.). Upper Saddle River, NJ: Prentice Hall.

Response to intervention: Policy considerations and implementation (2005). Alexandria, VA: National Association of State Directors of Special Education.

Ritchie, D., & Dunnick Karge, B. (1996). Making information memorable: Enhanced knowledge retention and recall through the elaboration process. *Preventing School Failure, 41,* 28-33.

Rowe, M. (1986). Wait time: Slowing down may be a way of speeding up! *Journal of Teacher Education, 37* (January-February), 43-49.

Rowe, M. (1983). Getting chemistry off the killer course list. *Journal of Chemical Education, 60,* 954-56.

Senjnost, R., & Thiese, S. (2001). *Reading and writing across content areas.* Andover, MA: Skylight.

Short, K., Harste, J., & Burke, C. (1996). *Creating classrooms for authors and inquirers* (2nd ed.). Portsmouth NH: Heineman.

Sousa, D. (2001). *How the brain learns.* Thousand Oaks, California: Corwin Press.

Stiggins, R., & Guskey, T. (2007). Assessment for learning: An essential foundation of productive instruction. In D. Reeves (Ed.), *Ahead of the curve: The power of assessment to transform teaching and learning.* Bloomington, Indiana: Solution Tree.

Sylwester, R. (1990). *A celebration of neurons: An educator's guide to the human brain.* Alexandria, VA: ASCD.

Taba, H. (1967). *Teacher's handbook for elementary social studies.* Reading, MA: Addison-Wesley.

Tomlinson, C., & McTighe, J. (2006). *Integrating differentiated instruction and understanding by design.* Alexandria, VA: ASCD.

Tomlinson, C. (2007/2008). Learning to love assessment. *Educational Leadership, 65* (December 2007/2008), 8-13.

Tompkins, G. (1998). *50 literacy strategies.* Upper Saddle River, NJ: Merrill.

Wagner, B. (1976). *Dorothy Heathcote: Drama as a learning medium.* Washington, D.C.: National Education Association.

Wilhelm, J. (2002). *Action strategies for deepening comprehension.* New York: Scholastic.

Wolfe, P. (2001). *Brain matters.* Alexandria, VA: ASCD.

Wormeli, R. (2005). *Summarization in any subject.* Alexandria, Virginia: ASCD.

Zike, D. (2004). *Big book of United States history for middle school and high school.* San Antonio, Texas: Dinah-Might Adventures.